BOWLING:
Ten Keys To Success

BY FRED BORDEN

Written by

Jay Elias

Graphic Design and Illustration by

Kim Garvin

Library of Congress Cataloging-in-Publication Data pending

©1991 by Fred Borden

Published, Printed and Distributed in the
United States of America
by Bowling Concepts, Inc.,
Akron, OH

Bowling: Ten Keys to Success

Table of Contents

Introduction i

    About This Book i

Chapter One

Promoting Safe and Courteous Bowling 1-1

    Overview 1-1

    Tips for Safer Bowling 1-1

        Avoid Moisture on Your Shoes .1-1

        Bowling Ball Safety 1-2

        Common Sense is the Key 1-2

    Basic Warmup Exercises to Prevent Injury 1-3

        Quadriceps 1-4

        Triceps 1-4

        Forearm Extenders 1-5

        Forearm Flexors 1-5

        Neck/Shoulder Stretch 1-6

        Neck Stretch 1-6

Calf Stretch 1-7

Side Stretch 1-7

Knee/Thigh Stretch 1-7

Achilles Stretch 1-8

Toe Touch 1-8

Bowling Center Etiquette 1-8

Who Bowls First? 1-9

Don't Wait: Just Do It! 1-9

Practice Restraint 1-10

Take Care of Your Bowling Center 1-10

Chapter Two

The Stance: Prepare to Perform 2-1

Overview 2-1

Where to Line Up 2-1

Distance From Foul Line 2-2

Lining Up to the Right or Left 2-3

Body Position: Waist Down 2-3

Feet 2-3

Knees 2-4

Body Position: Waist Up 2-4

Spine 2-4

Shoulders 2-5

Arms 2-6

Where to Hold the Bowling Ball 2-6

How to Hold the Bowling Ball 2-6

Wrist 2-8

Bowling Balance **2-8**

Chapter Three

The Approach: Four Steps to Success 3-1

Overview **3-1**

Four Steps to the Foul Line **3-1**

Step One: Position 1:1 3-2

Step Two: Position 2:2 3-3

Step Three: Position 3:3 3-3

Step Four: Position 4:4 3-4

Overview of Release and Follow-Through **3-5**

Where to Aim **3-6**

Troubleshooting Problems in Accuracy **3-6**

Avoid the Door Syndrome 3-6

Avoid the Rocking Chair Syndrome 3-8

Avoid Drifting 3-8

The Five Step Approach **3-9**

Chapter Four

The Armswing: A Closer Look 4-1

Overview 4-1

The Armswing: Front-to-Back View 4-1

Stay Inside the Pro Groove 4-2

Watch that First Step 4-3

The Armswing: Side View 4-3

Chapter Five

The Release 5-1

Overview 5-1

Review of Suitcase Release 5-1

Review of Release Timing 5-2

Maintain Your Hand Position 5-3

Beware of the Flippy Flops 5-3

Maintain Your Wrist Position 5-5

The Straight Ball 5-5

Chapter Six

The Finish Position 6-1

Overview 6-1

The Slide 6-1

The Follow-Through 6-2

Finish Position: Side View 6-4

Finish Position: Back-to-Front View 6-4

Chapter Seven

Making Spares: Easy as 1-2-3 7-1

Overview 7-1

Lane Basics 7-2

    Locator Dots 7-2

    Target Arrows 7-2

    Relationship to Pins 7-3

    Pin Numbering System 7-4

Step One: Determine the Key Pin Position 7-5

    Example One 7-5

    Example Two 7-6

    Example Three 7-6

Step Two: Align Your Feet 7-7

    Shots Right of Head Pin 7-7

    Shots Left of Head Pin 7-7

Step Three: Align Your Target 7-8

Shoulder Alignment When Making Spares 7-8

Walk Straight to Foul Line 7-9

Step One: Determine the Key Pin Position 7-12

    Example One 7-12

    Example Two 7-13

    Example Three 7-13

Step Two: Align Your Feet 7-14

    Shots Left of Head Pin 7-14

    Shots Right of Head Pin 7-14

Step Three: Align Your Target 7-15

Shoulder Alignment When Making Spares 7-15

Walk Straight to Foul Line 7-16

Chapter Eight

Adjusting to Lane Conditions 8-1

    Overview 8-1

    Consistency Comes First 8-1

    Lane Conditions 8-2

    How Lane Conditions Affect Your Game 8-2

    Dialing-In to Lane Conditions 8-3

        Move in Direction of Error 8-4

        Go With the Flow 8-5

Chapter Nine

Choosing the Right Equipment 9-1

Overview 9-1

Bowling Ball Basics 9-1

Ball Grip 9-2

Fit of Finger/Thumb Holes 9-2

Fit in the Hand 9-3

Types of Grips 9-3

Ball Cover 9-4

Ball Weight 9-5

Ball Weight in General 9-5

The Weight Block and Weighting 9-5

Right/Left Side Weight 9-6

Thumb/Finger Weight 9-7

Bowling Shoes 9-8

Chapter Ten

Mastering the Mental Game 10-1

Overview 10-1

Competence = Confidence 10-1

Make Bowling Fun! 10-2

Positive Self Talk 10-2

Positive Mental Imagery 10-2

    Why Imagery Works 10-3

    Practicing Imagery 10-3

Relaxation and Breathing 10-4

Mentally Preparing for a Game 10-5

Afterword

Where to Go from Here i

National Bowling Organizations i

Further Development iii

Appendix A

Keeping Score . . . . a-i

Basics of Scoring . . . . a-i

The Scorecard .a-ii

    Symbols Used on the Scorecard . . . . a-iii

The Tenth Frame . . . . a-iv

Scoring a Sample Game . . . . a-vi

300: The Perfect Game . . . . a-viii

Appendix B

Leagues and Tournaments . . . . b-i

Joining a League . . . . b-i

The Handicap System . . . . b-ii

Handicap, Scratch and Bracket Tournaments . . . . b-iv

Introduction

This book is dedicated to all bowlers who want to progress and realize a greater enjoyment of the sport.

Since the rise of the Egyptian Empire over 6,000 years ago, bowling — in one form or another — has captivated the masses as a diversion in which anyone can excel. Although kings have tried to abolish it and others have tried to demean it, bowling has outlived them and thrived all the stronger.

Today, there are more that 100 million bowlers in 90 countries throughout the world. In the United States alone, there are 71 million people who bowl at least once a year. Seven million of these are league bowlers who bowl in one or more weekly leagues.

Any individual, regardless of size, can compete successfully and enjoy this great sport. All it takes is understanding some key principles, practice, dedication and a positive mental attitude geared toward success.

Soon you will discover that bowling is more than a competitive sport. It offers a unique opportunity to socialize, relax and make new friends in a wholesome, fun-filled atmosphere. You will become part of a worldwide community of people who share a common love for this great sport.

About This Book

This book is primarily intended for beginning bowlers, though even experienced bowlers will benefit from the basic principles we explain.

These principles have been proven successful during thousands of bowling clinics and televised programs throughout the world. They are the product of over 30 years of testing and refinement. An individual who wants to improve can learn the game and become a successful competitor simply by understanding and practicing the keys we explain.

If you have never bowled before or are very new to the game, you may wish to read the following sections first:

- **Chapter Nine**: Chapter Nine explains how to select a bowling ball and the right type of shoes to wear. Although we strongly recommend not purchasing any equipment initially, this chapter will help you select correct bowling balls and shoes when you rent them at the bowling center.

- **Appendix A**: This section explains how to keep score in bowling and defines common bowling terms such as frames, strikes, spares and open frames.

- **Appendix B:** Perhaps the most exciting part of bowling is playing in a league. The comraderie and friendly competition make learning to bowl a truly enjoyable experience.

Many new bowlers fear they may not be good enough to join a team. The beauty of bowling is that any person can compete effectively in a sanctioned league. This is because of the handicap system. The handicap system gives newer bowlers with lower averages a "head start" by giving them handicap points before the game even starts.

Appendix B will explain how to get in a league, the different leagues you can join, the benefits of league membership and how the handicap system works.

For those who want to learn more advanced bowling techniques and truly excel in the sport, we strongly recommend, **Bowling: Knowledge is the Key**, also by Fred Borden. Although the subject matter is advanced, all principles are explained in simple English. This book covers in-depth such topics as advanced physical adjustments and releases, reading lanes, advanced lane play, and bowling ball weights. It is the perfect complement to **Bowling: Ten Keys to Success**.

Chapter One

Promoting Safe and Courteous Bowling

Overview

You are no doubt anxious to start improving your bowling skills. And that's what we're going to explore in just a few pages.

But first we want to discuss some basic points that will make your visits to the bowling center safe and enjoyable from the beginning.

First, we will give you some safety tips to make sure your visits to the bowling center are fun and safe. We will also show you some stretching and loosening exercises that will limber your body prior to bowling, promote smoother physical movement and help prevent injury.

Then, we will briefly cover a few basics of bowling etiquette. Remembering these do's and don'ts will prevent embarrassment and possible hurt feelings.

Tips for Safer Bowling

According to the United States Consumer Product Safety Commission, there are approximately 17,000 cases annually of bowling-related injuries that require hospital treatment. Since over 70 million people bowl a year, the chances of injury is actually very small compared to other sports, but accidents still happen. Bowling is a sport. As with all other sports, injury may result if basic safety practices are not followed.

Avoid Moisture on Your Shoes

Moisture is probably your number one enemy when bowling. The smooth rubber and leather on bowling soles get sticky when even slightly wet. This can be treacherous on the approach.

On rainy or snowy days, don't leave the bowling area more than necessary. Be sure to keep food and beverages out of the bowling area. Instead, enjoy refreshments in the concourse, lounge and snack bar areas. And watch where you walk whenever you leave the bowling area. Remember, the moisture you deposit on the approach is a hazard for your teammates as well as you.

Sometimes, new bowling shoes stick to the approach even when they are dry. Don't make the mistake of many bowlers and use baby powder on your soles. This can make them too slippery and will also create a hazard for other bowlers. Instead, use a knife and some sandpaper to round and smooth the leading edge of the heel of your sliding shoe. In extreme cases, placing a piece of teflon tape to the leading edge of your heel will correct the problem.

Bowling Ball Safety

It sounds silly to say, "Don't drop the ball on your foot," but many great bowlers accidentally have done just that. A bowling ball is a smooth, heavy object that can easily slip from your grasp if you're not careful. Before you pick up a bowling ball, always dry your hands with a towel or use the air blowers on the ball return.

When you pick up a ball from the return, grasp the ball from the sides. This prevents pinched fingers in case another ball comes zipping out. (See Figure 1-1.)

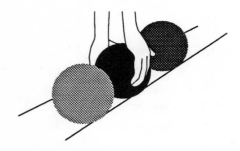

Figure 1-1

Don't put your fingers in the ball when you are picking it up and carrying it. Conserve the strength in your right hand and fingers for actual bowling. Instead, after you pick up the ball, cradle it in your left arm, as in Figure 1-2. (If you bowl left-handed, cradle the ball in your right arm.)

Figure 1-2

Be careful when lifting your bowling bag. Many bowlers carry two or more bowling balls in their bags. With the addition of shoes, wrist aids, other equipment and the weight of the bag itself, the combined weight can be over fifty pounds. When lifting your bag out of the car, keep your back straight, bend at the knees and waist, and use the big muscles of your legs to lift. Also, keep the weight of the bag close to your body.

Common Sense is the Key

Obviously, the best way to prevent injuries is to remain aware of what is going on around you and use simple common sense.

After bowling a shot, make sure to walk back on your side of the approach. Some people tend to watch their shots as they walk backward from the foul line. Drifting to the right or left is a good way to get in another person's way.

Basic Warmup Exercises to Prevent Injury

If people viewed bowling as a sport requiring proper strength and conditioning, the number of bowling-related injuries would probably be significantly reduced. While some injuries are caused by accidents, many others are the result of strain and stress on the body that builds up over time. This is called **microtrauma**. In bowling, microtrauma builds up in the shoulder, elbow, wrist and hand.

The principal cause of microtrauma is lack of pre-bowling warmup. Performing some simple warmup exercises just before bowling will limber your muscles and joints, prepare your body for maximum physical performance and help prevent injury.

The following loosening up exercises are designed to especially limber those areas that are used the most during bowling. We recommend performing three sets of five repetitions for each exercise.

These exercises are most effective when they are performed once or twice daily, and especially just before bowling.

Note: The following exercises have been taken from the YABA coaching manual **Beyond the Beginner**, also by Fred Borden.

Quadriceps

Balance on one leg while grasping foot of other leg and stretching it back to the opposite buttock. Alternate with other leg. This will stretch the front leg muscles. See Figure 1-3.

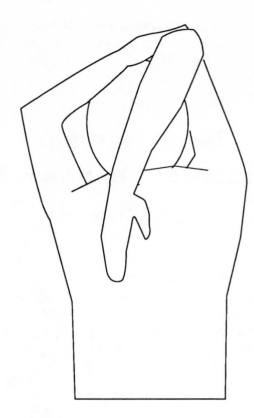

Figure 1-4

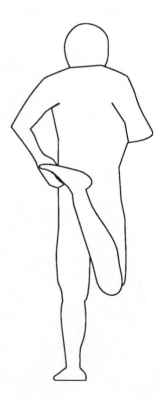

Figure 1-3

Triceps

Lift elbow of one arm over head (with rest of arm lowered). Grasp elbow with opposite hand and pull gently toward middle of head. Alternate with other arm. See Figure 1-4.

Forearm Extenders

Extend arm with hand bent downward at the wrist. Grasp fingers with other hand. Pull toward body. Repeat with other hand. See Figure 1-5.

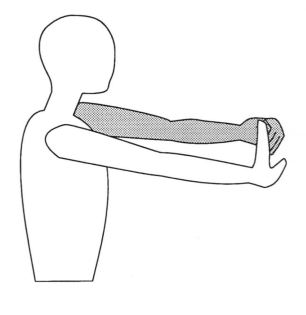

Figure 1-6

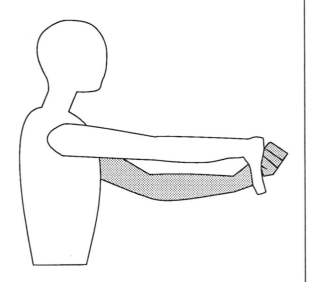

Figure 1-5

Forearm Flexors

Extend arm, with palm facing out and hand bent upward at the wrist. Grasp fingers with other hand. Pull toward body. Repeat with other hand. See Figure 1-6.

Neck/Shoulder Stretch

Bend head down. Slowly rotate head in a clockwise, then counterclockwise, motion. See Figure 1-7.

Neck Stretch

Move chin toward Adam's apple until you can feel tension on back of neck. See Figure 1-8.

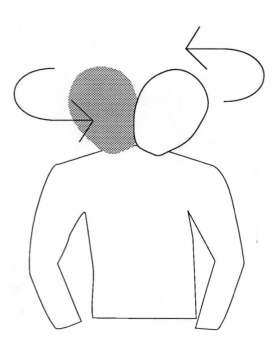

Figure 1-7

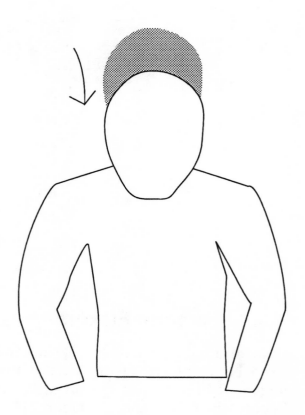

Figure 1-8

Calf Stretch

Balance balls of feet on stair (or step to approach and ball return). Lower and raise body at the ankle. See Figure 1-9.

Figure 1-10

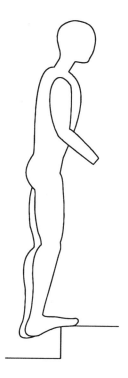

Figure 1-9

Side Stretch

Extend right arm over head, while keeping other arm at side. Bend sideways at the waist toward left side. Alternate with other side. See Figure 1-10.

Knee/Thigh Stretch

Place your left leg in back and your right leg in front of your body. By bending your right knee and extending your left leg, shift your weight forward and hold. Alternate leg position and repeat. See Figure 1-11.

Figure 1-11

Toe Touch

Cross legs. Bend body at waist, moving fingers as close as comfortable toward toes. Hold. Alternate position of feet and repeat. See Figure 1-13.

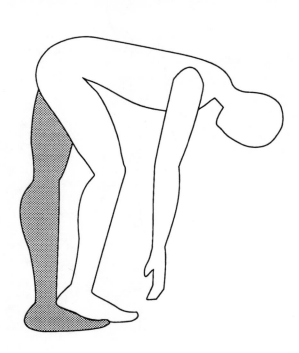

Figure 1-13

Figure 1-12

Achilles Stretch

Place palms up against a wall. Place your left leg in back and your right leg in front of your body. Stretch out your left leg while bending your right knee until you feel tension, and hold. Repeat with legs alternated. See Figure 1-12.

Bowling Center Etiquette

When you go to bowl, you expect to have a good time. That means enjoying the companionship of your friends, relaxing in the pleasant atmosphere of the bowling center and getting some good exercise while developing your skills.

Nothing can spoil a great attitude faster than having an annoying person next to you. You have a right to be treated with respect. If you are like most of us, your free time is rare and therefore valuable. You expect to be able to enjoy yourself during the occasional breaks from your busy schedule.

Respect works both ways. You must first treat others with respect in order to receive it.

Who Bowls First?

When you get up to bowl, and there are two people on either side of you, who should bowl first? The general rule is: the first one up should go first. If there is **any question who was the first** to get up, the **person to the right should bowl first**.

Don't Wait: Just Do It!

Another guideline to remember is that **once you are lined up in your stance, don't wait, just go**. Many people get in the stance, fidget for awhile until they feel they have it right, then stare in fixation at the pins for a minute or more.

You can't stare the pins down! If you want to knock them down, you have to throw the ball!

During fast-paced competition people get annoyed quickly with a person who hesitates in the stance. Moreover, as we will cover later, hesitation does not promote a proper mental game. People who hesitate in the stance tend to "over-think" and end up getting "pysched out."

The time for thinking about a shot is **before you line up in the stance**. Once you step up on the approach, the time for thinking is over. **Just do it!**

And if the lanes are crowded and others are waiting to bowl, don't wait at the foul line to see what you are going to get.

Adopting these guidelines will help promote a fast-paced game and make the evening more exciting.

Practice Restraint

Obviously, in the heat of competition, emotions and enthusiasm run high. And that's one of the things that makes bowling such a great sport.

Just make sure your enthusiasm doesn't hinder or irritate those around you. Obviously, your enthusiasm about making three strikes in a row will not be appreciated by those next to you if you run over into their lane whooping and hollering.

Be especially considerate toward your teammates. Part of the comraderie of friendship is taking — or giving — a little ribbing from time to time. But don't get carried away and make jokes at the expense of others. Again, treat people the way you would want to be treated.

Bowling is a wholesome family sport, so don't use profanity in the bowling center. Do have a good time, but try not to be overly loud or rowdy.

Avoid negative mental attitudes. Throwing temper tantrums or becoming glum and moody will do more than aggravate your teammates. Negative mental attitudes will adversely affect your performance.

Take Care of Your Bowling Center

Caring for a bowling center is everyone's responsibility, not just the proprietor's. Remember: the condition of a bowling center reflects on the public perception of bowlers and bowling as a sport.

If you smoke, be careful not to burn furnishings and floor coverings. Put chewing gum where it belongs. Clean up your spills and dispose of all trash in waste receptacles.

When you are visiting other bowling centers, respect their rules. Though the rules may not be the same as you are used to, complying with them is simply a matter of good manners. Remember: "When in Rome .... "

Chapter Two

The Stance: Prepare to Perform

Overview

Imagine a sprinter dropping down into the track blocks and preparing to run. Or a baseball player getting up to bat. A golfer lining up for a shot. A football lineman dropping into a three-point stance.

In each of these examples, an athlete is preparing the body to perform. Though the positions vary according to the sport, each athlete assumes a stance that will translate into top performance when it comes time to move.

In bowling, a correct stance is just as important as in any other sport. A bowler is an athlete preparing to perform a series of precise athletic movements. The body must be located at the correct spot in a well-balanced, comfortable position.

In this chapter we will cover the two basic aspects of the stance:

- where to line up;

- how to line up.

If you are new to bowling, the points we will cover may seem like a lot to remember at first. After the first few times, though, you'll notice that a correct stance simply **feels right**. Soon, your body will naturally assume a proper stance without any conscious thought.

Where to Line Up

There are two things to consider when determining where to line up:

- distance from the lane;

- positioning to the right or left.

On the approach, there are marks that help you determine where to line up: the **foul line** and **locator dots**. Figure 2-1 shows where these are on the lane.

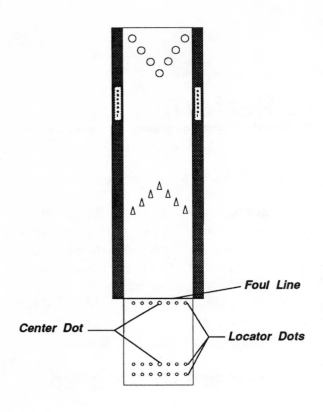

Figure 2-1

Distance From Foul Line

As a general rule, a person five feet tall would want to line up on the second set of locator dots from the foul line. This will vary, though, according to your height. A taller person will want to line up farther away than a shorter person. This is because a taller person has a longer stride.

Here is a simple method to precisely determine how far away to line up.

1. Line up facing **away** from the lane with your heels approximately two inches from the foul line.

2. If you are right-handed, start with your right foot and take 4 1/2 **brisk steps**. If you are left-handed, start with your left foot and take 4 1/2 **brisk steps**.

    The four steps take into account the four steps for the approach. The extra half step is for the slide at the end. It will also give you some leeway so you don't go over the foul line.

3. Pivot on the foot in front of you so you are facing the lane. This is where you should line up.

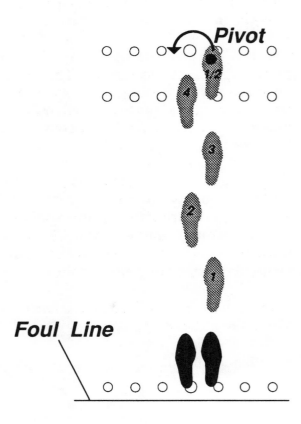

Figure 2-2

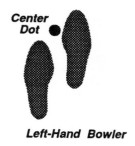

Left-Hand Bowler

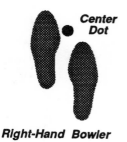

Right-Hand Bowler

The Stance: Position to the Right or Left

Figure 2-3

Lining Up to the Right or Left

If you are **right-handed,** line up with the **left foot an inch or so to the left of the center dot.**

If you are **left-handed,** line up with the **right foot an inch or so to the right of the center dot.**

When practicing, move back and forth in the stance one inch at a time until you find the spot that is perfect for you.

This is the basic position where you will line up when making strikes (trying to knock down all ten pins at the same time). Later in this book we will teach you how to shift this position back and forth to make spares (knocking down the remaining pins after the first try). We will also show how to adjust this position to compensate for the condition of the lane (whether its oily, medium or dry).

Body Position: Waist Down

Feet

If you bowl **right-handed,** position your **right foot about five inches in back of your left foot.** This will give you a better base. Also, it will help you start easier during the approach, since you will be moving your right foot first.

If you are **left-handed,** position your **left foot about five inches in back of your right foot.**

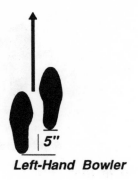 

Left-Hand Bowler   **Right-Hand Bowler**

Figure 2-4

Knees

When you line up in the stance, **flex your knees slightly**. After all, you are an athlete preparing to execute a series of fluid movements. Avoid locking your knee joints. Instead, bend and relax them.

How far? We recommend that you tilt your knees forward 10- 15° so they extend out toward the toes 4-6".

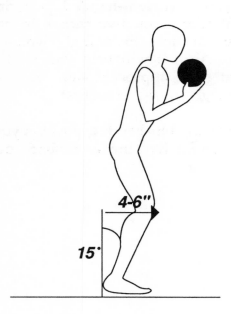

Figure 2-5

How would you bend your knees if you were catching a bag of potatoes dropped from a truck? This is a good mental picture of how to position yourself.

Be sure to keep your knees flexed throughout the approach without straightening up.

Body Position: Waist Up

Spine

When it comes time to bowl, you are going to be moving forward. To help prepare yourself, the weight of your body should be positioned forward.

Tilt your spine forward approximately 15°. Make sure you maintain this position throughout the approach and delivery.

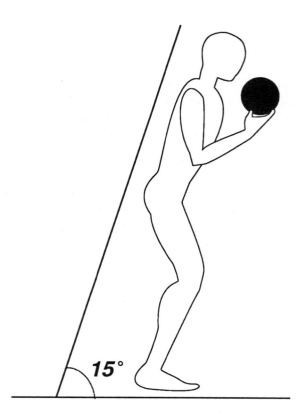

Figure 2-6

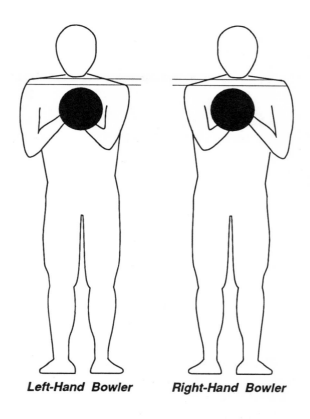

Left-Hand Bowler   *Right-Hand Bowler*

Figure 2-7

Shoulders

When you bowl, the weight of the ball is on one side of your body. It's only natural that the weight of one shoulder will be a little lower than the other.

If you bowl **right-handed**, let your **right shoulder drop a couple inches lower than the left. If you bowl left-handed, allow your left shoulder to drop a couple inches lower than the right.**

It's been said that we could all bowl better if our eyes were on top of our shoulder. Then we could see the path of the ball precisely.

We can still develop good mental pictures of this. We call the path the ball takes down the lane the **Target Line** or the **Line in Your Mind.**

When you bowl, imagine a three foot arrow resting on your shoulder. Align this three foot arrow with the target line.

**Picture the
"LINE IN YOUR MIND"**

Figure 2-8

Arms

Make sure the elbow of your bowling arm is resting against your side when holding the ball. The other hand should help cradle and support the ball in the stance.

Figure 2-9

Where to Hold the Bowling Ball

You've probably noticed that some bowlers hold the ball at chest level, while other bowlers hold it at hip level or below.

Both of these positions — and any in between — are correct. Where you hold the ball depends upon how fast you get to the foul line in the approach. The **faster you are, the lower you hold the ball**. This will help synchronize the armswing to your footsteps during the approach.

A **slow** bowler should hold the ball at **chest level**. A **medium speed** bowler should hold the ball at **waist level**. A **fast bowler** should hold the ball **below the waist**.

Experiment with different positions until you find the one that is right for you.

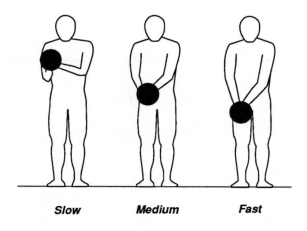

Slow   Medium   Fast

Figure 2-10

How to Hold the Bowling Ball

In the stance, the weight of the ball should rest against the pincher muscles of your bowling hand.

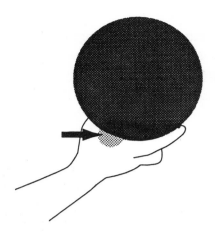

Figure 2-11

As we mentioned earlier, the other hand should help support the weight of the bowling ball. The little finger of each hand should touch.

You may have a question about what fingers go in what holes. Your thumb goes into the hole that is larger than the other two holes and is apart from them. Place your middle finger and ring finger in the other holes as in Figure 2-12.

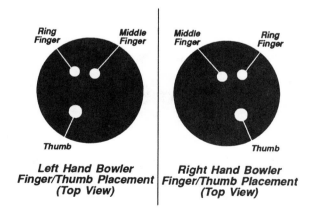

Left Hand Bowler
Finger/Thumb Placement
(Top View)

Right Hand Bowler
Finger/Thumb Placement
(Top View)

Figure 2-12

In Chapter Five we will show you different ways to position the ball in your hand, but for now we want to discuss the easiest one for beginners: the "suitcase."

Imagine you were holding the handle of a suitcase. This is how you would position your hand when holding the bowling ball. The suitcase delivery is also referred to as the "money shot" because your thumb faces your pants pocket during the armswing.

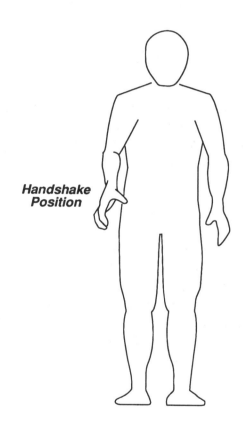

*Handshake
Position*

Figure 2-13

A third way to visualize this is to imagine the face of a clock around your bowling ball. If you are right-handed, your thumb should be in the 10:00 position. If you are left-handed, place your thumb in the 2:00 position.

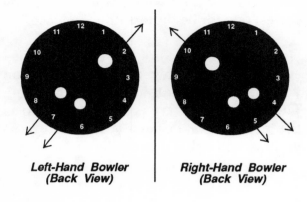

Figure 2-14

It is important to maintain this hand position throughout the approach and delivery. When you throw the ball, imagine that you are shaking hands with the pins.

Wrist

Keep your wrist straight during the release. You may notice that some advanced bowlers cup their wrist to give the ball more spin, or break the wrist to make the ball go straighter. This is an **advanced technique you should only try after mastering the basics.**

Make sure your wrist remains in the same position throughout the approach and delivery.

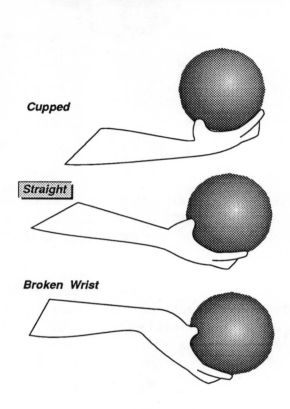

Figure 2-15

Bowling Balance

If you follow all the guidelines we have just explained, you should feel relaxed, balanced and natural in the stance.

When in the stance, your weight should be balanced on the balls of your feet. Just before you begin your approach, rock back

on your heels very slightly, then forward
as you begin to take your first step.

   This rocking motion should not be notice-
able to the eye but just enough so that you
can feel it.

=====================

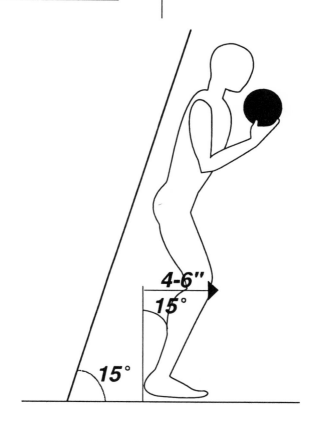

Chapter Three

The Approach: Four Steps to Success

Overview

The most inspiring sight in bowling is a true professional performing during the approach. A proper approach combines agility, speed, form, coordination, timing and accuracy. All muscles in the body function in unison to send a 16 pound ball on its precise course to the pins.

Although it may sound difficult at first, anyone can realize success. Mastering the approach first takes knowledge (which we will give you in this chapter). Then it takes lots of practice to train the muscles to perform what the mind already knows.

In this chapter we will first break down the approach step-by-step. Then we will briefly describe the release and follow-through so you will have enough information to go out and start practicing. After this, we will discuss some common problems in the approach that affect accuracy and give you the keys to cure these problems. Finally, we will briefly discuss the five step approach some bowlers use.

Although we break down the approach into four basic steps, they should be performed as one fluid motion. A successful approach occurs when the body and mind work as one in a free-flowing series of coordinated movements.

Four Steps to the Foul Line

Although there are different types of approaches, the most common is the four step approach. This is the approach we recommend.

We will number each footstep, then relate this to the position of the bowling ball at the end of each step.

There are five separate positions we will cover. The first is the stance position. We call this the 0:0 position.

Figure 3-1

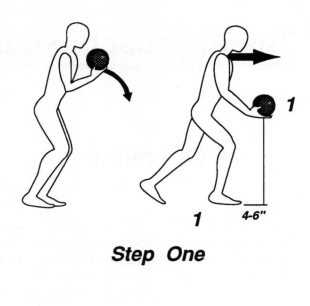

Step One

Figure 3-2

In Figure 3-1 the position of the right foot is numbered 0 and shown in relation to the ball position, which is also numbered 0.

Step One: Position 1:1

During the first step, the right foot steps forward as the right arm pushes the ball out and down toward the right foot simultaneously. At the end of the first step, the ball should be poised above the right foot. The left hand should continue to help support the ball throughout this step.

Note: If you bowl left-handed, move your left foot forward as the left hand pushes the ball out toward the lane and over the foot.

Two points are important to remember during this step:

1. Make sure that the leg and arm move at the same time. If the ball and foot don't end up in the 1:1 position simultaneously, your timing will be off throughout the approach.

2. Move the ball straight out toward the lane so that it ends up over your

right foot. Don't let it veer to the right or left.

Often we refer to this as the **pushaway**, because you should push the ball out toward the lane and down toward the floor.

Step Two: Position 2:2

During the second step the left foot moves forward as the ball arcs down. The left hand should leave the ball at the beginning of the step. At the end of the second step, the ball should end up beside the right calf.

Note: **If you bowl left-handed,** during the second step the right foot moves forward as the ball arcs down. The right hand should leave the ball at the beginning of the step. At the end of the second step, the ball should end up beside the left calf.

Step Three: Position 3:3

During the third step the right foot moves forward as the ball arcs back to the highest point of the armswing. This should be about shoulder height.

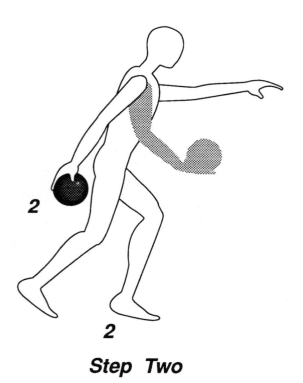

Step Two

Figure 3-3

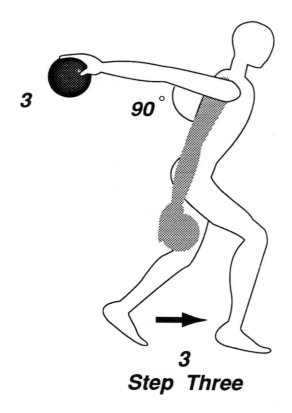

Step Three

Figure 3-4

Note: **If you bowl left-handed**, move your left foot forward as the ball arcs back to the height of the backswing.

Step Four: Position 4:4

During the fourth step the left foot should step forward into the slide as the ball arcs down. At the end of the fourth step, the ball should be in the lowest part of the armswing. The right arm should be pointed directly at the floor.

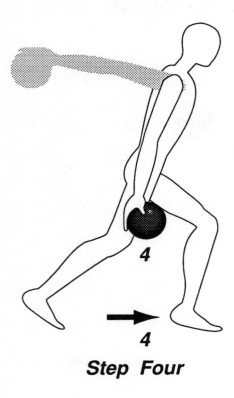

4

4

Step Four

Figure 3-5

Note: **If you bowl left-handed**, move your right foot forward and plant for the slide while the ball arcs down.

After the fourth step you should continue through the release and follow-through without hesitation.

As the ball starts down during the fourth step, your right foot should slide sideways in back of your left leg. Simultaneously, you should "sit down" or lower your knees slightly and position your weight slightly back so you end up in a comfortable sitting position with the lower body and the spine tilted 15° forward.

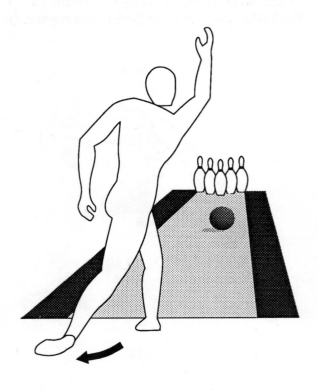

Figure 3-6

Note: **If you bowl left-handed**, your left foot should slide sideways in back of your right leg.

Make sure you do not slide over the foul line during the fourth step. If you slide over the foul line during competition (and release the ball), you receive no points for the shot.

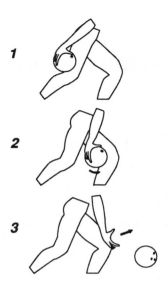

Figure 3-7

Overview of Release and Follow-Through

In Chapters Five and Six we will cover the release and follow-through in detail. That's chapters away, however, and you probably want to start bowling before then. Here are a few basic points about the release and follow-through.

A release occurs in three steps:

1. Just after the fourth step, the **thumb should release from the ball**. If you are still holding the ball correctly in the suitcase position, the thumb should drop out of the ball naturally.

2. The **fingers** (which are still in the holes) should continue to **lift out and up**. With the hand in the suitcase position, this should impart a natural sideways spin to the ball, causing it to hook slightly into the pins.

3. The **fingers should release smoothly** from the ball as your hand continues arcing out and up in the follow-through.

You should end up in the finish position with your hand still aligned with the Target Line.

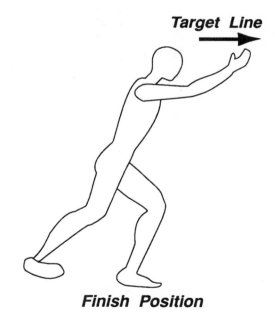

Target Line

Finish Position

Figure 3-8

Where to Aim

Although we will cover taking aim in later chapters, you are probably anxious to practice and want to know where to aim for a strike. Figure 3-9 shows a bowling lane. Notice that there are seven arrows on the lane. These are called **Target Arrows**. The arrows are numbered from right-to-left if you bowl right-handed, or from left-to-right if you bowl left-handed.

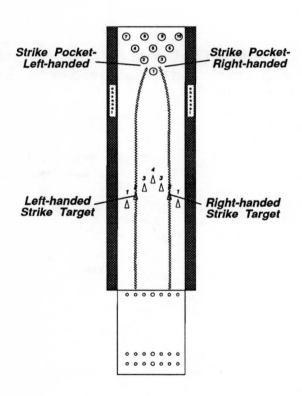

Figure 3-9

For now, aim for the second target arrow. Using the suitcase release, the ball should hook into the side of the #1 pin (head pin). We call this area the **strike pocket**, because this is the **best place to hit the pins to make a strike**.

If your shot consistently misses a little to the right, move a little to the right in the stance. If it misses a little to the left, move a little to the left.

We will cover taking aim for strikes and spares extensively in Chapters Seven and Eight of this book.

Troubleshooting Problems in Accuracy

Although we will cover other keys to accuracy in the next two chapters, perhaps the biggest factor is the position of the shoulders.

As we said in Chapter Two, imagine a three-foot arrow balanced on the shoulder of your bowling arm and aligned with the Target Line your ball will follow down the lane. Make sure your shoulders remain aligned with this Target Line in the stance, throughout the approach and during the release and follow-through.

Avoid the Door Syndrome

We often refer to the shoulders in relation to the lane. Shoulders can be either opened or closed in relation to the lane. If the shoulders are open, they are **turned away from the center pin**. If the **shoulders are closed**, they are **turned toward the center pin**.

We want the **shoulders nearly perfectly square to the lane**. This position should be adopted in the stance and maintained throughout the approach and delivery. (See Figure 3-10.)

Remember:

- **Open Shoulders = Ball Out**. For right-handed bowlers, the ball will miss to the right. (For left-handers, the ball will miss to the left.)

- **Closed Shoulders = Ball In**. For right-handed bowlers, the ball will miss to the left. (For left-handers, the ball will miss to the right.)

Often the problem of opening or closing the shoulders is a matter of improper timing. Problems with timing usually begin with the first step of the approach.

For Right Hand Bowlers

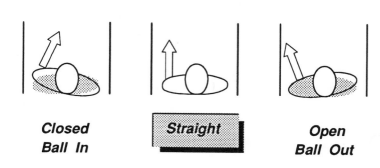

For Left Hand Bowlers

Figure 3-10

If your armswing is slower than your feet, your arm will end up in the backswing when you take the fourth step. This contorts your body. The result is that your shoulders will be open and pointed out during the release. Your ball will miss to the right if you are right-handed. If you are left-handed, your ball will miss to the left.

The opposite happens if your armswing is faster than your feet. When this occurs, the ball is released before the end of the fourth step. Your body ends up twisted, with the shoulders closed in relation to the lane. This means that the ball will miss to the left if you are right-handed. The opposite will hold true if you are left-handed.

We have a saying: "A great start equals a great finish."

Most timing problems can be cured during the first step. Make sure to move your hand and foot as one during the first step.

If you still have problems timing your armswing to your feet movements, **try raising or lowering the ball in the stance**. Remember what we discussed in Chapter Two:

• If your **armswing is faster than your feet movements**, raise the ball in the stance to **chest level**.

• If your **armswing is slower than your feet movements**, lower the ball in the stance to **waist level**.

Avoid the Rocking Chair Syndrome

Some bowlers have a problem rocking their shoulders forward and backward during the approach. This results in erratic ball behavior and inaccurate bowling.

If the shoulders rock forward during the fourth step and release, the ball will impact before the foul line, bounce back up, and hit the lane again. We call this a "double dribble."

If the shoulders rock back during the fourth step and release, the ball will be lofted far out onto the lane. A little loft on the ball is good, but only in small doses.

The cure is to keep your spine tilted in the same 15° angle as in the stance.

A good mental picture is to imagine balancing a cup of coffee on your shoulders. Try not to spill a drop during your approach and delivery.

Avoid Drifting

Be careful not to drift to the right or left with your feet during the approach. Drifting is another major cause of inaccuracy. Check where your feet are located after a shot. You should end up with your feet **within one or two boards of where you lined up in the stance**.

The locator dots where you line up are lined up with the locator dots behind the foul line. This means if you line up in the stance with your left foot beside the center dot, you should end up with your left foot beside the center dot at the foul line.

As with an inaccurate armswing, drifting is often caused by improper timing. If the armswing is not properly timed to the footsteps, the body will not be balanced properly. This results in the body drifting right or left. Review the keys to proper timing in this chapter if you experience drifting.

The number one reason for drifting, though, is the armswing. If the arm wraps in behind your body, you will drift left. If the arm swings out away from your body, you will drift right.

Keep in mind that accuracy is not possible unless the armswing is straight. In the next chapter, we'll cover the armswing in even greater detail.

The Five Step Approach

You may have heard about the five step approach. The five step approach is the same as the four step approach except that there is an initial "getting started" baby step at the beginning. The ball does not move from the stance position during this initial step.

If you bowl right-handed, this small getting started step will be with the left foot. If you bowl left-handed, the getting started step will be with the right foot.

After the baby step, the Five Step Approach is the same as the Four Step Approach.

Note: If you use the five step approach, make sure to give yourself more room from the foul line to allow for the extra baby step.

Chapter Four

The Armswing: A Closer Look

Overview

When we discuss the armswing, we are really talking about accuracy. Keeping the arm on line and developing a consistent armswing are the two keys to accuracy.

Notice the emphasis we place on **consistency**. Developing consistency in your game is the first requirement to becoming a truly great bowler.

Consistency is more important in the armswing than in any other area of bowling. As you will soon learn, where you line up in the stance will vary. How you hold the bowling ball may vary. But your armswing should never vary.

In this chapter we will analyze the armswing from two views: the **front-to-back** view and the **side view**. Using the front-to-back perspective, we'll show the importance of maintaining your armswing in the narrow **pro groove**. Then we will investigate the side view and the importance of developing a **smooth pendulum swing** that is consistent time after time.

The Armswing: Front-to-Back View

To visualize the front-to-back view, imagine that your are standing inside the face of a clock.

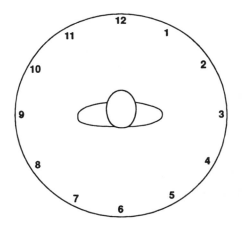

Figure 4-1

Directly in front of you would be 12:00. Just to the right of you would be 1:00. Directly behind you would be 6:00, and just to the right of this would be 5:00.

If you bowl right handed, during the armswing you want to:

1.   Push the ball out between 12:00 and 1:00 during the pushaway.

2.   Arc the ball back between 5:00 and 6:00 during the backswing.

3.   Arc the ball forward between the 12:00 and 1:00 position during the forward swing and delivery.

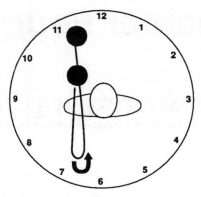

Left-handed Armswing

Figure 4-3

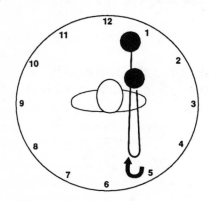

Right-handed Armswing

Figure 4-2

If you bowl left-handed, during the armswing you want to:

1.   Push the ball out between 12:00 and 11:00 during the pushaway.

2.   Arc the ball back between 7:00 and 6:00 during the backswing.

3.   Arc the ball forward between the 12:00 and 11:00 position during the forward swing and delivery.

Stay Inside the Pro Groove

Notice that there is a slight looping action during the armswing. The emphasis here is that the motion is **slight: no more than two inches either way.**

We call this narrow four inch slot the **Pro Groove.** Keep yourself **inside the pro groove to achieve consistent accuracy.**

Observe other bowlers during the backswing. Some bowlers tend to wrap the bowling arm in back of them during the backswing. This will make the ball go out to the right (when bowling right-handed). Remember this key to trouble-shooting your game:

•   **Arm In = Ball Out.**

Arm In = Ball Out

Figure 4-4

Other bowlers let the ball bounce out away from them in the backswing. This will make the ball go in to the left (when bowling right-handed). The key to remember here is:

* **Arm Out = Ball In.**

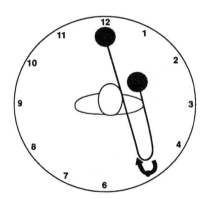

Arm Out = Ball In

Figure 4-5

Watch that First Step

As we mentioned earlier, an inaccurate armswing is often caused by pushing ball to the right or left during the first step. Push the ball out straight and down toward the right foot during the first step and your armswing will get off to a good, straight start.

Also remember that improper timing can throw your armswing off.

* If your **armswing is faster than your feet, the ball will go in**. This is because your arm reaches the release point before your feet, closing your shoulders in relation to the lane.

* If your **armswing is slower than your feet, the ball will go out**. This is because your feet reach the release point before your arm, opening your shoulders in relation to the lane.

Make sure your foot and arm move together during the first step. Also experiment with raising or lowering the ball in the stance to correct timing problems.

The Armswing: Side View

Figure 4-6 shows the armswing from the side view.

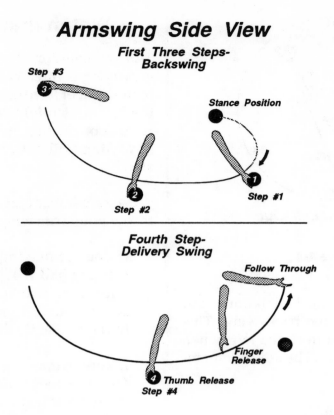

Armswing Side View

First Three Steps-
Backswing

Step #3

Stance Position

Step #1

Step #2

Fourth Step-
Delivery Swing

Follow Through

Finger
Release

Thumb Release
Step #4

Figure 4-6

All footsteps have been numbered to show how the movements of the feet correspond to a properly timed armswing.

Notice that the backswing goes up to about shoulder height. It is important to keep the height of your armswing consistent. This will promote consistent timing.

From the backswing, the arm arcs down toward the floor, then back up and through to the finish position. Imagine an airplane coming in for a landing, then taking off again just before touching the ground. This is what a proper forward swing resembles.

Notice we have also shown the points of thumb release and finger release. The thumb releases at the lowest point of the armswing, just after the fourth step. The fingers release as you begin arcing up toward the finish position. Since the fingers are on the side of the ball, this translates into sideways spin and hook potential.

In the finish position the arm should be raised with the hand pointing toward the ceiling.

Chapter Five

The Release

Overview

Some new bowlers have difficulty with the release. Perhaps this is because there are many different types of releases used by bowlers. A beginning bowler will often become confused, or try to adopt more advanced releases before mastering the simple ones.

Also, new bowlers often fear that they will drop the bowling ball prematurely. The forward momentum of the bowling ball, however, usually keeps it firmly against the hand until it's time to release it.

When performed properly, **the release should occur naturally.** The holes on a bowling ball are drilled in such a way to encourage a good release with the thumb and fingers dropping out of the holes at the proper time.

In this chapter we will review the Suitcase release we briefly covered in Chapters Two and Three. We will also review proper timing during the release.

Then we will cover solutions to two common problems bowlers experience with the release: turning the hand over the ball to try to force the hook and flipping the thumb out (the backup ball).

Finally, we will explain a second basic release that's good to know: the straight ball release.

Review of Suitcase Release

As we mentioned earlier, to perform a suitcase (handshake) release, put the thumb in the 10:00 "handshake position" in the stance. Then maintain this position throughout the approach and release.

If you bowl left-handed, put your thumb in the 2:00 position and maintain it throughout the approach and release.

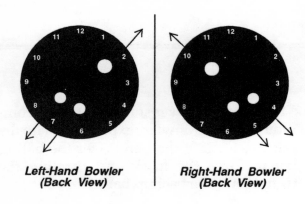

Left-Hand Bowler
(Back View)

Right-Hand Bowler
(Back View)

Figure 5-1

Develop a mental picture of reaching out and shaking hands with the second target arrow. This should help keep the thumb in the correct position.

Review of Release Timing

If you are holding the ball naturally and your thumb and fingers fit comfortably in the holes (not too tight and not too loose), the thumb should drop out of the ball at the

end of the fourth step. This is the lowest point of the delivery swing.

After the thumb drops out, the fingers remain in the ball while lifting out and up toward the finish position. Since the fingers are on the side of the ball, this natural lifting action will impart sideways spin on the ball.

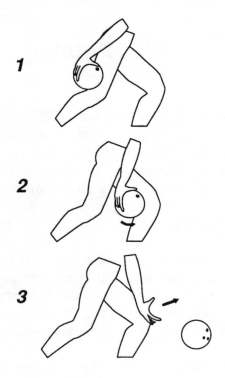

Figure 5-2

Under medium lane conditions (not very oily or very dry), this spinning action will make the bowling ball hook into the strike pocket.

Maintain Your Hand Position

Some bowlers try to force the hook by turning the hand up over the ball at the moment of release. It is important to maintain the same hand position from the moment you line up in the stance until you end up in the finish position.

There is really no need to flip the ball to generate spin and hook on the ball. As we just mentioned, the action of the fingers lifting on the side of the ball will impart the sideways spin necessary for the hook.

Although there are some advanced releases that involve cocking the hand in the stance, then uncocking it during the release, these are best left to experienced bowlers who have mastered the basics.

Beware of the Flippy Flops

Some bowlers have a problem with a **backup ball** or reverse curve. A backup ball ends up curving away from the center head pin and toward the channel.

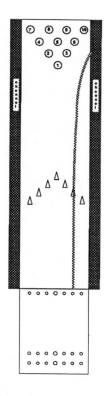

Figure 5-3

A backup ball occurs because the thumb opens out during the release. The weight of the ball sometimes causes a bowler to flop the hand open, making the thumb flip out away from the bowler instead of pointed toward the pants pocket in the 10:00 position.

Some bowlers compensate for a backup ball by lining up differently in the stance and angling the shoulders in relation to the lane. This only partially takes care of the problem. Even if the backup ball hits the strike pocket, the improper angle of the shot will result in a low percentage of strikes.

If you experience problems with the back-up ball, remember to keep the thumb pointed in towards your pants pocket throughout the approach and release.

Note: If you try to maintain your thumb position, but still have problems with a backup ball, you can try the "I changed my mind," method. Line up with your thumb open and out if you want. Then right at the moment

of thumb release, change your mind and flip your thumb back towards your pants pocket. (See Figure 5-4.)

(This is actually one of the advanced releases used by the professionals. Some people, though, find it simpler if they are having problems with a backup ball.)

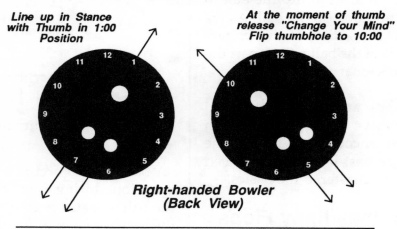

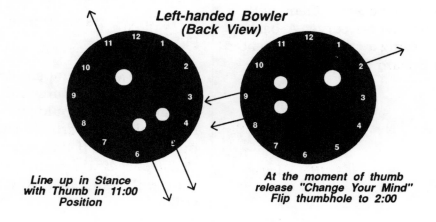

Figure 5-4

Maintain Your Wrist Position

In Chapter Two we mentioned the three types of wrist positions: Broken, Straight and Cupped.

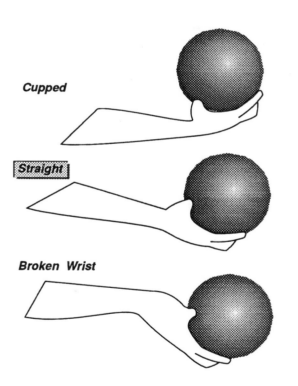

Cupped

Straight

Broken Wrist

Figure 5-5

We recommend that newer bowlers **use a straight wrist**, although any wrist position is acceptable. What is important, however, is to make sure that the **wrist remains in the same position** in the stance and throughout the approach, release and follow-through.

The Straight Ball

Although the suitcase release is probably the best for new bowlers because it is simple and promotes proper hook and angle, the straight ball release is good for certain situations.

For example, if the lanes are very oily and the ball won't hook (or the lanes are very dry and the ball is hooking extremely), you probably want to go for a straighter game. Also, a straight ball is great for picking up difficult spares where accuracy is critical.

To bowl a straight ball, point your thumb straight up toward the ceiling, (the 12:00 position) in the stance. Maintain this position throughout the approach, release and follow-through.

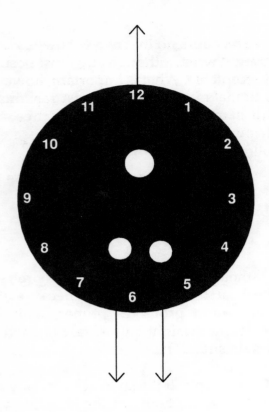

Figure 5-6

During the slide, the thumb should release from the ball first. As the fingers lift out and up, the ball will simply roll from the fingers and onto the lane. This promotes a good rolling action on the lane.

Note: Since with a straight ball there will be little if any hook on the ball, right-hand bowlers will want to line up a few boards farther to the right in the stance.

Left-hand bowlers will want to line up a few boards farther to the left.

Although a straight delivery is more accurate than a suitcase delivery, keep in mind that your percentage of strikes will not be as high. This is because there is no hook on the ball and you will not be hitting the strike pocket at the proper angle.

Chapter Six

The Finish Position

Overview

Many people wonder why the Finish Position is so important. After all, the ball has already been released and is on its way down the lane. There is nothing more that a bowler can do to influence the outcome.

The reason why the finish position is important is moving into the finish position will promote a **correct follow-through.**

Think about throwing a football. If a quarterback's hands stopped at the moment the football was released, speed, distance and accuracy would be sacrificed. If a tennis player stopped the arm an instant after connecting, the tennis ball probably wouldn't clear the net.

A correct follow-through and finish position will help you maintain accuracy, body balance and consistent success.

In this chapter we will first review the **slide,** which actually **begins just before ball release.** Then we will break down the different parts of the **follow-through.** Finally, we will evaluate the **finish position** from a side view and from a back-to-front view.

The Slide

As you will recall, at the end of the fourth step the left foot plants for the slide. At the same time the right foot should slide sideways in back of the body.

If you are left-handed, plant the right foot for the slide while you slide the left foot in back of your body.

Moving the foot in back of the body does three things:

- It helps move the hip inside to allow more clearance for the bowling ball as it moves past.

- It provides a broader base to promote better balance during the release and follow-through.

- It shifts the weight of the body toward the side opposite the bowling ball for better balance.

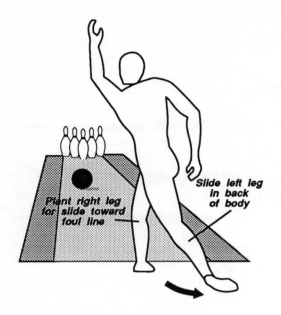

**Finish Position
Left-hand Bowler**

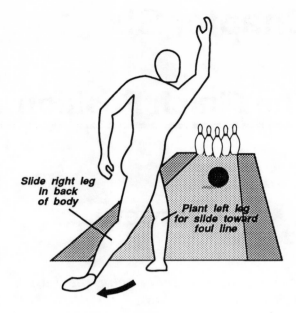

**Finish Position
Right-hand Bowler**

Figure 6-1

Also, flex your knees a little more during the slide. This promotes better ball delivery onto the lane and also gives you better balance.

The Follow-Through

Two main points are important to remember during the follow-through:

• Lift the arm out and up.

• Keep the body down.

Let's break this down. As the ball rolls from your fingers, your arm should continue to arc upwards toward the ceiling. Also, the hand should remain aligned with the Target Line that the ball will follow down the lane. In the case of a strike ball, your hand would be pointed at the second target arrow.

At the same time, the body should be kept low. This does not mean to bend down. Remember in Chapter Three we discussed the Rocking Chair Syndrome and the problems that result if the body bends over more or rears up during the release.

Instead, **bend with the knees** and shift the weight of your body back slightly. When performed properly, it feels comfortable, like sitting back in a chair. Simply keep your spine tilted 15° forward, flex your knees and let the ball roll right off your fingers as you lift up toward the ceiling.

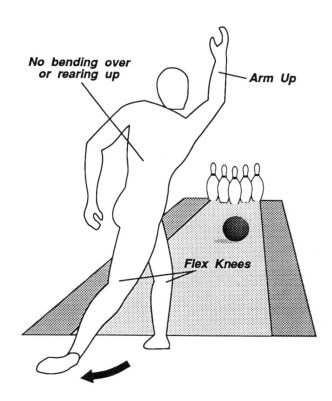

Figure 6-2

Finish Position: Side View

Figure 6-3 shows a side view of the Finish Position that shows what we just discussed. In the perfect finish position, your head, knee and toe should be aligned in a straight line perpendicular to the floor.

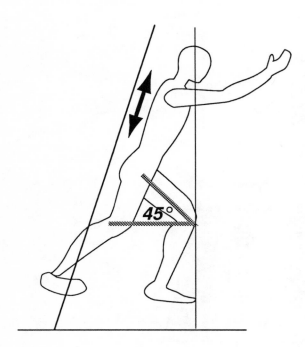

Figure 6-3

Notice that:

- The arm has continued arcing upward after ball release.

- The angle of the spine is the same as it was in the stance. No rocking chair syndrome.

- The knees have flexed further to complement a better delivery of the ball onto the lane.

Finish Position: Back-to-Front View

Figure 6-4 shows the back-to-front view of the Finish Position.

For a right-handed bowler the right arm should end up at approximately the 1:00 position, with the left leg at 6:00, the right leg at 7:00 and the head at 12:00.

For a left-handed bowler the left arm should end up at approximately the 11:00 position, with the right leg at 6:00, the left leg at 5:00 and the head at 12:00.

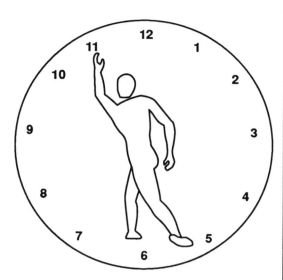

**Finish Position
Left-hand Bowler**

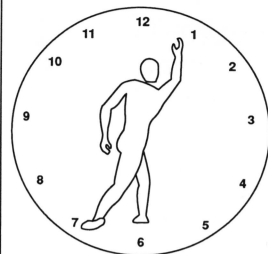

**Finish Position
Right-hand Bowler**

Figure 6-4

Chapter Seven

Making Spares: Easy as 1-2-3

Overview

Now we are going to talk about the way to increase your score faster than anything else: making spares.

Every time it's your turn to bowl you have two chances to knock down all the pins. These two chances are referred to as a **frame**.

If you knock down all the pins the first time, you get a **strike** and you don't have to bowl your second shot.

If you don't knock down all the pins the first time, you get a second chance. This is called a **spare**. If you don't make a spare, it's called an **open frame**.

The quickest way for a new bowler to get up to a 170 average score or higher is to make all the spares. In bowling, when you make a spare, this is called a **spare conversion**.

The art of making spares is often called **math bowling**. Although the term may seem imposing, the only math you really need to know is addition and subtraction.

Making a spare is as simple as 1-2-3.

1. Determine which **Key Position** to hit to make the spare.

2. **Line up your feet** in the proper position.

3. Aim for the **correct target**.

In this chapter we will first discuss some lane fundamentals and basic terms you need to know. Then we will break down how to make spares from a right-hand and left-hand bowling perspective.

Note: To make the material easier to understand, the end of this chapter is broken down into two separate sections for right-handed and left-handed bowlers. After reading the **Pin Numbering** Section, please refer to either **The 1-2-3's of Making Spares: Right-Hand Bowler** or **The 1-2-3's of Making Spares: Left-Hand Bowler**.

Lane Basics

The first thing to know about a bowling lane is that **all lanes are created equal**. Every lane in the world is the same width and the same length. The boards are spaced the same distance apart (about one inch). And the locator dots and target arrows are always in the same place.

The second thing to know is that the **locator dots, target arrows and key out-side pins of the pin triangle all line up.**

Locator Dots

Refer to Figure 7-1. Notice that there are three sets of locator dots before the foul line. Each dot is spaced five boards from the next. **All three sets of locator dots line up with each other**.

Note: There is also a set of locator dots after the foul line. The set of dots after the foul line **do not** line up with the three sets before the foul line. The dots after the foul line are used by advanced bowlers as "rear gun sights" to fine-tune the angle precisely.

Target Arrows

As we said in Chapter Three, there are seven target arrows 15 feet out on the lane.

The **arrows on the right side** are for **right-handed bowlers**, and the **arrows on the left side** are for **left-handed bowlers**.

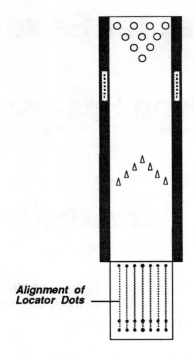

Alignment of Locator Dots

Figure 7-1

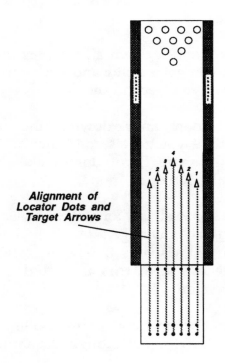

Alignment of Locator Dots and Target Arrows

Figure 7-2

The target arrows are **numbered right-to-left** for **right-handed bowlers** and **numbered left-to-right** for **left-handed bowlers**.

We are mainly concerned with the second and third target arrows. You aim at one of these arrows (or sometimes the space between them) when making spares.

Notice that the **target arrows are in line with the locator dots**. The center locator dot corresponds to the center target arrow and so on.

Relationship to Pins

Refer to Figure 7-3.

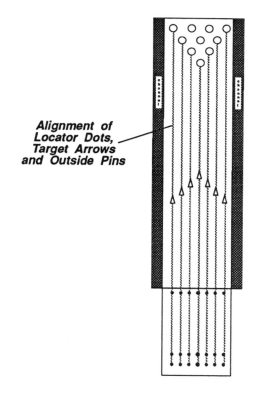

Alignment of Locator Dots, Target Arrows and Outside Pins

Figure 7-3

Notice how the Target Lines are also lined up with the key outside pins. By **outside pins**, we mean **the seven pins forming the "V" that is pointed toward you**. We also refer to these seven pins as the **Key Pin Positions**. Remember: **Any spare can be made by simply aiming at one of the seven Key Pin Positions**.

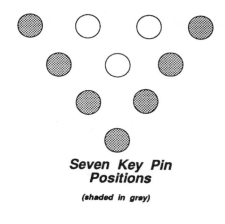

Seven Key Pin Positions

(shaded in gray)

Figure 7-4

Why are these called target arrows? Because **the target arrows are what you aim for!** The **target arrows mirror the location of the key pin positions**. It's much easier to aim for a target that is 15 feet instead of 60 feet away.

In summary, the following are all in line with each other:

• the three sets of locator dots;

• the target arrows;

• the key pin positions.

Pin Numbering System

There are ten pins in the pin triangle. They are numbered according to Figure 7-5. The **seven key pin positions are shaded in gray**.

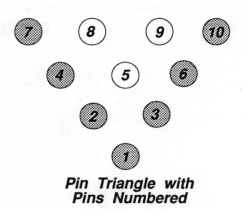

Pin Triangle with Pins Numbered

Figure 7-5

To remember the pin numbers, simply start with the head pin as number one, then count from left to right.

In the rest of this chapter we will refer to the pins by number.

Note: If you are a left-handed bowler, please skip the following section and read **The 1-2-3's of Making Spares: Left- Hand Bowler**.

The 1-2-3's of Making Spares: Right-Hand Bowler

Step One: Determine the Key Pin Position

There are literally hundreds of possible spare combinations you might be faced with. Does this mean that you have to memorize hundreds of different shots?

It's actually much simpler because **every shot is a one pin shot!**

Remember: **Any spare can be made by aiming for the proper key pin position.**

A few examples should help clear this up.

Example One

A common spare is the #4-#7.

To make this shot, you would aim for the #4 pin. The ball will strike the #4 pin which will knock into the #7 pin. It's a domino effect.

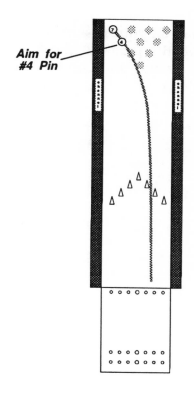

Figure 7-6R

This sample demonstrates a good rule of thumb: **The key pin you want to aim for is usually the pin closest to you.**

Example Two

Sometimes, no key pins are left standing. When this is the case, you want to do a **make-believe shot**. In other words you would aim for where the key position pin was standing.

Let's say on your first shot you knocked down all the pins but the #5. What key position would you aim for? The #1 pin. Actually, you would aim the same as you would for a strike.

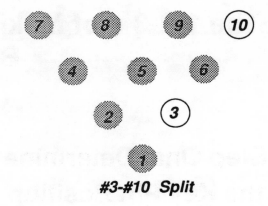

#3-#10 Split

Figure 7-8R

In this example, you would not aim for either the #3 or the #10. If you did hit one, the other would still be standing. Instead, you would want to aim between them, or where the #6 pin had been standing, as in Figure 7-9R.

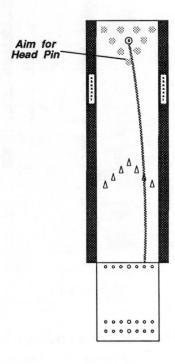

Figure 7-7R

Example Three

Another common spare is the #3-#10 split, also called the baby split. (When one or more balls are left standing, and there is a gap between them, the spare is called a split.)

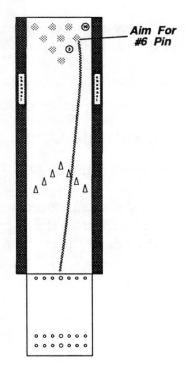

Figure 7-9R

Step Two: Align Your Feet

The next step is to move to either right or left of where you line up for a strike shot. For **shots to the right of the head pin, move left;** for **shots to the left of the head pin, move right.**

Note: When making the #1 and/or #5 pin, stay in your strike position without moving right or left.

Shots Right of Head Pin

For **shots to the right of the head pin, move your stance position left four boards at a time.**

In other words:

• For #3 pin spares, move left four boards from where you line up for a strike.

• For #6 pin spares, move left eight boards.

• For #10 pin spares move left 12 boards.

Shots Left of Head Pin

For **shots to the left of the head pin, move your stance position right in three board increments.**

In other words:

• For #2 pin spares, move right three boards from where you line up for a strike.

• For #4 pin spares, move right six boards.

• For #7 pin spares move right nine boards.

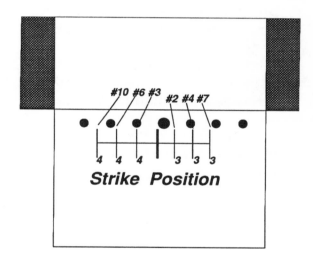

Strike Position

Figure 7-10R

Note: You may wonder why you move four boards at a time for shots to the right, and three boards at a time for shots to the left. This is because you are throwing against the rotation of the ball when you make spares to the right and with the rotation of the ball when you make spares to the left.

Step Three: Align Your Target

In Chapter Three we briefly mentioned that when making a **strike shot** you should **aim for the second arrow**.

This changes when you are making spares. As you shift over in the stance to make the spare, the target arrow you aim for will also change. Sometimes, you will be aiming between the target arrows.

- For **#1 and #5 pin spares**, do not change your target. **Use the second target arrow** as you would for a strike.

- For **all spares to the left of the head pin, aim between the second and third target arrows.**

- For **#3 pin spares, also aim between the second and third target arrows.**

- For **#6 and #10 pin spares, aim at the third target arrow.**

Shoulder Alignment When Making Spares

As your position in the stance and your target changes, so will the angle of your body in relation to the lane.

Remember in Chapter Two we discussed how shoulders could be either opened, closed or straight in relation to the lane. We also said that for strike shots, your shoulders should be straight in relation to the lane.

When making spares, this is not always true. What is true is that you should **always point your body in the direction of the target.**

We call this **presetting the angle of the shoulders.** Remember these three rules:

- When making #1 and #5 position spares, keep your shoulders straight in relation to the lane, just as you would when making a strike.

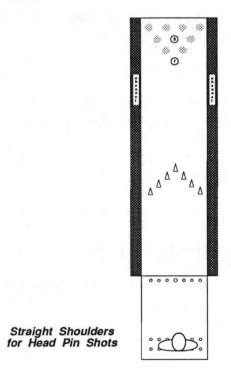

Straight Shoulders for Head Pin Shots

Figure 7-11R

- When making **shots to the right** of the head pin, **open your shoulders** in relation to the lane.

- When **making shots to the left** of the head pin, **close your shoulders** in relation to the lane.

Doing this is easy if you once again imagine that three foot arrow poised on your right shoulder. Simply point that arrow on your **right shoulder at the target and your angle will automatically be correct.**

Note: Some new bowlers change their armswing out or in when aiming at an angle to the lane. **Never change your armswing.** Instead, **change the angle of your shoulders.**

Walk <u>Straight</u> to Foul Line

Even though your shoulders may be angled open or closed toward the lane, remember this very important point:

- **Always walk straight toward the foul line.**

This means that you should never drift right or left or walk at an angle in relation to the lane.

If your shoulders are open or closed, you want to **walk slightly on the sides of your feet** so that you end up with your feet on the same boards they were on in the stance.

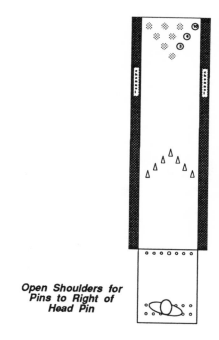

Open Shoulders for Pins to Right of Head Pin

Figure 7-12R

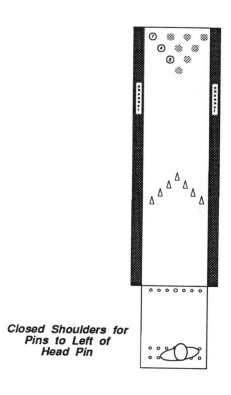

Closed Shoulders for Pins to Left of Head Pin

Figure 7-13R

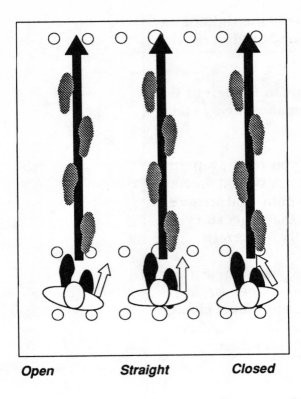

Open   **Straight**   **Closed**

Figure 7-14R

Note: Drifting to the right is particularly a problem with the #10 shot. This is because your angle in relation to the lane is sharp, and it is difficult to walk straight to the foul line.

If you have a problem making the #10 pin, check your feet in the stance and at the foul line. Make sure that you drift no more than one or two boards.

The following spare chart summarizes many of the points that we covered in this section. It may be helpful to refer to it the next few times you bowl.

Right-Handed Spare Conversion Chart

Spares Right of Head Pin

Feet
Move 4 Boards Left for Each Pin Right of Head Pin.

Target

#3 Pin:
Aim Between 2nd and 3rd Arrows.

#6 Pin:
Aim at 3rd Target Arrow.

#10 Pin:
Aim Between 3rd and 4th Target Arrows.

#3 Pin ————
#6 Pin ∞∞∞∞∞
#10 Pin - - - - -

Spares Left of Head Pin

Feet
Move 3 Boards Right for Each Pin Left of the Head Pin.

Target

Aim Between 2nd and 3rd Arrows.

#2 Pin ————
#4 Pin ∞∞∞∞∞
#7 Pin - - - - -

* #1 and #5 Pins Same as Strike Line.
* Note: Make all spare adjustments based upon your _adjusted_ strike position.

The 1-2-3's of Making Spares: Left-Hand Bowlers

Step One: Determine the Key Pin Position

There are literally hundreds of possible spare combinations you might be faced with. Does this mean that you have to memorize hundreds of different shots?

It's actually much simpler because **every shot is a one pin shot!**

Remember: **Any spare can be made by aiming for the proper key pin position.**

A few examples should help clear this up.

Example One

A common spare is the #6-#10.

To make this shot, you would aim for the #6 pin. The ball will strike the #6 pin which will knock into the #10 pin. It's a domino effect.

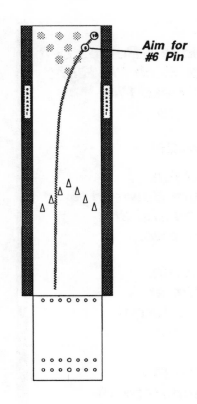

Figure 7-6L

This sample demonstrates a good rule of thumb: **The key pin you want to aim for is usually the pin closest to you.**

Example Two

Sometimes, no key pins are left standing. When this is the case, you want to do a **make-believe shot**. In other words you would aim for where the key position pin was standing.

Let's say on your first shot you knocked down all the pins but the #5. What key position would you aim for? The #1 pin. Actually, you would aim the same as you would for a strike.

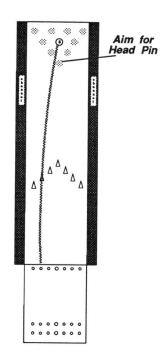

Figure 7-7L

Example Three

Another common spare is the #2-#7 split, also called the baby split. (When one or more pins are left standing, and there is a gap between them, the spare is called a **split**.)

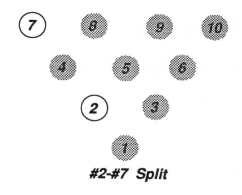

#2-#7 Split

Figure 7-8L

In this example, you would not aim for either the #2 or the #7. If you did hit one, the other would still be standing. Instead, you would want to aim between them, or where the #4 pin had been standing, as in Figure 7-9L.

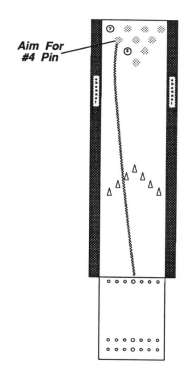

Figure 7-9L

Step Two: Align Your Feet

The next step is to move to either left or right of where you line up for a strike shot. For **shots to the left of the head pin, move right**; for **shots to the right of the head pin, move left**.

Note: When making the #1 and/or #5 pin, stay in your strike position without moving left or right.

Shots Left of Head Pin

For **shots to the left of the head pin, move your stance position right four boards at a time.**

In other words:

*   For #2 pin spares, move right four boards from where you line up for a strike.

*   For #4 pin spares, move right eight boards.

*   For #7 pin spares move right 12 boards.

Shots Right of Head Pin

For **shots to the right of the head pin, move your stance position left in three board increments.**

In other words:

*   For #3 pin spares, move left three boards from where you line up for a strike.

*   For #6 pin spares, move left six boards.

*   For #10 pin spares move left nine boards.

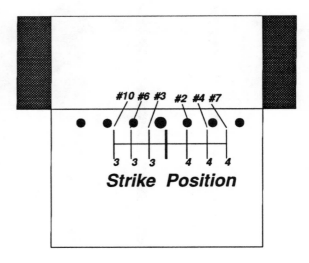

Figure 7-10L

Note: You may wonder why you move four boards at a time for shots to the left, and three boards at a time for shots to the right. This is because you are throwing against the rotation of the ball when you make spares to the left and with the rotation of the ball when you make spares to the right.

Step Three: Align Your Target

In Chapter Three we briefly mentioned that when making a **strike shot** you should **aim for the second arrow.**

This changes when you are making spares. As you shift over in the stance to make the spare, the target arrow you aim for will also change. Sometimes, you will be aiming between the target arrows.

- For **#1 and #5 pin spares**, do not change your target. **Use the second target arrow** as you would for a strike.

- For **all spares to the right of the head pin, aim between the second and third target arrows.**

- For **#2 pin spares, also aim between the second and third target arrows.**

- For **#4 and #7 pin spares, aim at the third target arrow.**

Shoulder Alignment When Making Spares

As your position in the stance and your target changes, so will the angle of your body in relation to the lane.

Remember in Chapter Two we discussed how shoulders could be either opened, closed or straight in relation to the lane. We also said that for strike shots, your shoulders should be straight in relation to the lane.

When making spares, this is not always true. What is true is that you should **always point your body in the direction of the target.**

We call this **presetting the angle of the shoulders.** Remember these three rules:

- When making #1 and #5 position spares, keep your shoulders straight in relation to the lane, just as you would when making a strike.

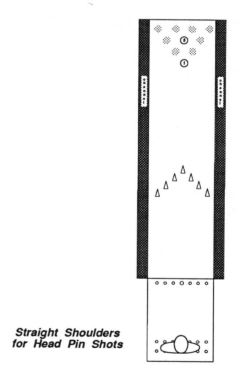

Straight Shoulders for Head Pin Shots

Figure 7-11L

- When making **shots to the left** of the head pin, **open your shoulders** in relation to the lane.

- When **making shots to the right** of the head pin, **close your shoulders** in relation to the lane.

Doing this is easy if you once again imagine that three foot arrow poised on your left shoulder. Simply point that arrow on your **left shoulder at the target and your angle will automatically be correct.**

Note: Some new bowlers change their armswing out or in when aiming at an angle to the lane. **Never change your armswing.** Instead, **change the angle of your shoulders.**

Walk <u>Straight</u> to Foul Line

Even though your shoulders may be angled open or closed toward the lane, remember this very important point:

- **Always walk straight toward the foul line.**

This means that you should never drift left or right or walk at an angle in relation to the lane.

If your shoulders are open or closed, you want to **walk slightly on the sides of your feet** so that you end up with your feet on the same boards they were on in the stance.

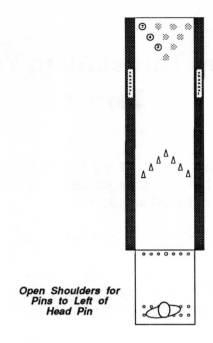

Open Shoulders for Pins to Left of Head Pin

Figure 7-12L

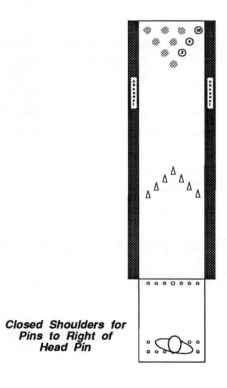

Closed Shoulders for Pins to Right of Head Pin

Figure 7-13L

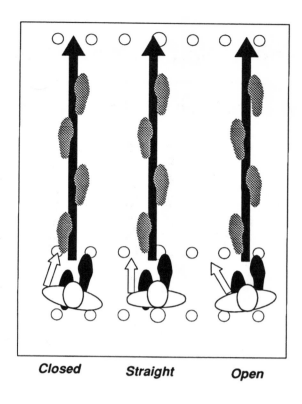

Closed   Straight   Open

Figure 7-14L

Note: Drifting to the right is particularly a problem with the #7 shot. This is because your angle in relation to the lane is sharp, and it is difficult to walk straight to the foul line.

If you have a problem making the #7 pin, check your feet in the stance and at the foul line. Make sure that you drift no more than one or two boards.

The following spare chart summarizes many of the points that we covered in this section. It may be helpful to refer to it the next few times you bowl.

Left-Handed Spare Conversion Chart

Spares Left of Head Pin

Feet

Move 4 Boards Right for Each Pin Left of the #1 Pin.

Target

#2 Pin: Aim Between 2nd and 3rd Arrows.

#4 Pin: Use 3rd Target Arrow.

#7 Pin: Aim Between 3rd and 4th Arrows.

#2 Pin ————
#4 Pin 〰〰〰〰
#7 Pin · · · · · ·

Spares Right of Head Pin

Feet

Move 3 Boards Left for Each Pin Right of the Head Pin.

Target

Aim Between 2nd and 3rd Arrows.

#3 Pin ————
#6 Pin 〰〰〰〰
#10 Pin · · · · · ·

* #1 and #5 Pins Same as Strike Line.
* Note: Make all adjustments based upon your _adjusted_ strike position.

Chapter Eight

Adjusting to Lane Conditions

Overview

You have probably noticed that the surface of a lane looks very shiny. At times your bowling ball may have come back with an oily ring around it. This is because lane conditioner is regularly applied to a lane. The conditioner helps protect the wood surface. It also allows the ball to initially skid on the lane surface before rolling and hooking into the pins.

As soon as the oil conditioner is applied to a lane it begins to evaporate. How fast the oil evaporates depends upon how much the lane is being used, overhead lighting, the porosity of the wood, the type of conditioner and other factors.

Lane conditioning is important because the amount of oil on a lane determines how your ball will react during a shot.

You may have noticed during a game that even though you were doing everything correct, you consistently missed to the right or left of the head pin.

The reason was probably because there was more or less oil conditioner on the lane than the last time you bowled.

The amount of oil is not the only consideration. Where the oil is located is also important. The condition of the lane itself is also a factor. If it has been some time since the lanes were refinished, areas have probably become old and worn. All these factors play a role on what your ball does once it leaves your fingers.

In this chapter we will first discuss the importance of developing a good, consistent physical game. Then we will cover the three main lane conditions and explain how lane conditions affect your bowling. Finally, we will show how to adjust to lane conditions.

Consistency Comes First

In order to determine the condition of the lane and adjust accordingly, you first must be able to determine if your physical game and timing feel proper. This means that your game must be consistent.

Adjusting to lane conditions is possible only if:

• You have an accurate, consistent armswing;

• Your armswing is timed properly with your feet movements;

• The release has been mastered and is the same every time;

• You walk straight to the foul line without drifting more than a board or two right or left.

Once you have developed consistency in your physical game, it is time to start considering the condition of the lane and how to adjust.

Lane Conditions

There are three basic types of lane conditions: **oily, medium and dry**. Think of these conditions as colors spread out on the lane: dry as red, medium as white and oily as blue. As soon as you get up to bowl, try to determine which of these three conditions exist.

Look at the lane. Can you detect patches of oil? Or are there dry, worn patches where the conditioner has evaporated? Check your ball when it comes back. Is there a telltale oily ring around it, or is it fairly dry?

How Lane Conditions Affect Your Game

Lane conditions affect the performance of your ball on the lane. This is why it is necessary to learn how to adjust.

If the lanes are dry, your ball will "dig in" more when it hooks. In other words, more of the sideways spin of the ball will be translated into hooking power.

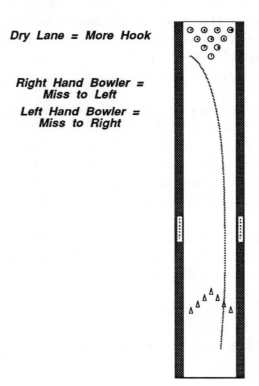

Dry Lane = More Hook

Right Hand Bowler = Miss to Left

Left Hand Bowler = Miss to Right

Figure 8-1

If you are right-handed, your ball will probably hook too far to the left. If you are left-handed, your ball will hook too far to the right.

If the lanes are oily, however, your ball will skid and slide more, and there will be little (if any) hook. This is because the ball cannot get the traction to hook.

Oily Lane = Less Hook

Right Hand Bowler = Miss to Right

Left Hand Bowler = Miss to Left

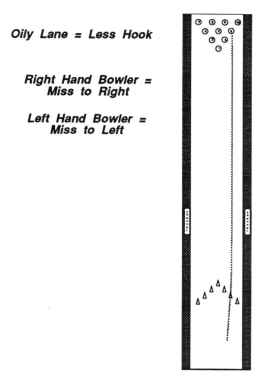

Figure 8-2

If you are right-handed, your ball will probably miss to the right. If you are left-handed, your ball will miss to the left.

If there is a medium amount of oil on the lane, no adjustments should be necessary. Just play your regular game.

Medium Lane = Medium Hook

No Adjustments Necessary

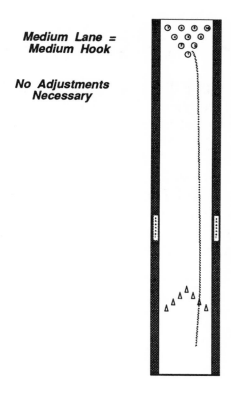

Figure 8-3

Dialing-In to Lane Conditions

We refer to adjusting to lane conditions as getting "dialed-in." In competition, the game often goes to the person who recognizes what's happening out on the lane and gets dialed-in first.

There are two basic guidelines for dialing-in to lane conditions:

1.   **Move in the Direction of the Error**

2. Go With the Flow

Move in Direction of Error

If your ball consistently **misses to the right, move to the right** in the stance. If your ball **misses to the left, move to the left.**

How far should you move? That depends upon how far your shots are off. If you are missing seven boards to the left, move over seven boards, then make fine adjustments from there to get dialed-in precisely.

Aim for the same target out on the lane. Just move to the right or left in the stance. This means that you will be **opening or closing your shoulders in relation to the lane.**

For **right-handed bowlers, open your shoulders** when you **adjust to the left,** and **close your shoulders** when you **adjust to the right.**

For **left-handed bowlers, close your shoulders** when you **adjust to the left,** and **open your shoulders** when you **adjust to the right.**

Dialing In: Right-hand Bowler

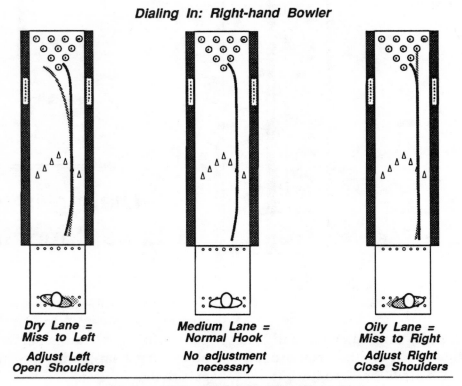

Dry Lane = Miss to Left
Adjust Left Open Shoulders

Medium Lane = Normal Hook
No adjustment necessary

Oily Lane = Miss to Right
Adjust Right Close Shoulders

Always Walk Straight to the Foul Line: No Drifting

Figure 8-4

Dialing In: Left-hand Bowler

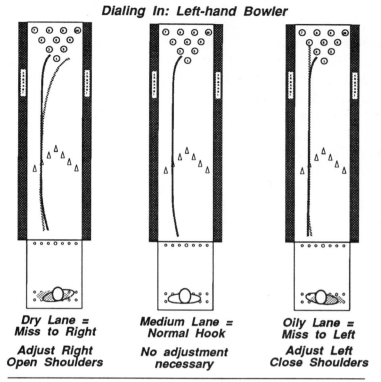

Dry Lane =
Miss to Right

Adjust Right
Open Shoulders

Medium Lane =
Normal Hook

No adjustment
necessary

Oily Lane =
Miss to Left

Adjust Left
Close Shoulders

Always Walk Straight to the Foul Line:
No Drifting

Figure 8-5

Remember: even though you are moving to the right or left **still walk straight to the foul line**. This means that sometimes you will want to walk slightly on the sides of your feet. Check your feet position in the stance and at the foul line to make sure you are not drifting to the right or left.

Go With the Flow

Going with the flow means to take full advantage of whatever lane condition is present. This means:

• **Play a Straighter Game When the Lanes are Oily.**

• **Play a Hook Game When the Lanes are Dry.**

How can you change your game? Remember in Chapter Six we mentioned two basic releases: the Suitcase Release and the Straight Ball Release.

When the lane conditions are dry, you are going to have a great hook. So take full advantage of this and use the Suitcase Release.

When the lane conditions are very oily, a hook ball is nearly impossible. Also, the sideways spin on the ball will make the ball skid more, meaning that you will lose the turn on the ball. So slow down and lay the ball down earlier, before the foul line. (The ball will not set off the foul light because it passes too quickly.) This will encourage more roll on the ball.

Note: In this chapter we have discussed basic methods of adjusting to lane conditions. More advanced methods of reading lanes and adjusting accordingly are covered extensively in **Bowling: Knowledge is the Key**.

Chapter Nine

Choosing the Right Equipment

Overview

For just about every sport, one or more pieces of equipment are necessary to participate. Obviously, in bowling your major piece of equipment is the bowling ball.

The first bowling balls were constructed nearly 7,000 years ago in Egypt and were made of stone. During the 17th, 18th and 19th centuries, balls were made from hard tropical wood or a laminate of different types of wood. In the early 1900's, the hard rubber ball was developed. Today's balls are constructed of rugged plastic polymers such as polyurethane and polyester.

A bowling ball is more than a heavy globe with three holes in it. Bowling balls are precisely weighted and drilled to provide comfort and perform in specific ways out on the lane.

The second most important pieces of equipment are your bowling shoes. Bowling shoes are designed to prevent scuff marks on the approach, provide traction and enable a good slide during the release. There are different types of bowling shoes for right-handed and left-handed bowlers.

In this chapter, we will discuss the basics of ball construction. Next we will cover the three most important points you should know about bowling balls: Grip, Cover and Weighting. Then, we will briefly discuss bowling shoes and show you how to tell the difference between shoes for right-handed and left-handed bowlers.

Bowling Ball Basics

A bowling ball is composed of three parts: the shell, core and weight block.

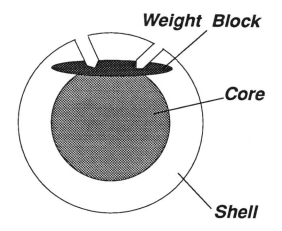

Figure 9-1

The **shell** is the outside covering of the ball. It is hard and durable to withstand landing on the lanes and impacting the pins. The **core** is the center of the bowling ball. On top of the core is a pancake-shaped piece of dense, heavy material. This is called the **weight block**. The weight block gives a bowling ball more weight on the top than on the bottom to allow for drilling of the thumb and finger holes.

Bowling balls are usually drilled with three holes for the thumb, middle finger and ring finger. (Actually, you are allowed to have one more hole drilled in a ball other than the thumb and finger holes. This is called a weight hole and is used by advanced bowlers for specific applications.)

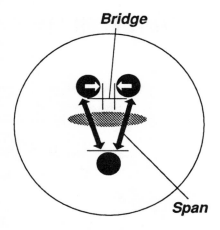

Bridge

Span

Figure 9-2

The distance between the two finger holes is called the **bridge**. The distance between the thumb hole and finger holes is called the **span**.

All bowling balls are 27" in circumference and approximately nine inches in diameter. The weight of a bowling ball varies from six to 16 pounds. According to ABC/WIBC regulations, a bowling ball cannot weigh more than 16 pounds.

There are various markings on the outside of a bowling ball. Usually there is the logo of the manufacturer, the brand name of the ball, a serial number and a small dot showing where the top of the weight block is located. Some people also have their names engraved on a bowling ball. On a house ball (provided by a bowling center), the weight of the ball will be marked above the finger holes.

Note: If you use house balls and do not have a bowling ball yet, remember that every ball has its own serial number. If you find a ball that works well for you, remember the serial number so you can find it the next time you bowl.

Ball Grip

Holes are drilled in bowling balls by ball drillers at the pro shop. These individuals are skilled specialists, many of whom have played professionally. A good ball driller will work with you to customize a ball that will fit you perfectly and complement the way you bowl.

Fit of Finger/Thumb Holes

You want the finger and thumb holes to be snug enough so you won't drop the ball, yet loose enough to afford a smooth release. The thumb hole should be a little looser than the finger holes, since the thumb drops out first during the release.

Note: If the holes are too big, you can place a strip of tape in the back of the holes to make them smaller. You can do this according to the weather. Usually, your hands are somewhat larger when it's warm outside and smaller when it's cold.

You may have heard people mention thumb and finger pitch. This refers to how the holes are drilled in relation to the center of the ball. A skilled ball driller will make sure that the pitch of the thumb and fingers are perfect for you and your game.

Fit in the Hand

The distance between the two finger holes (bridge) should be about a quarter inch.

The distance between the thumb hole and finger holes (span) depends upon the size of your hand and which type of grip you use. (We'll cover the types of grips shortly.) Comfort is the key. Notice the web of skin between your thumb and index finger. With a properly fitted ball the web should be neither taut nor slack.

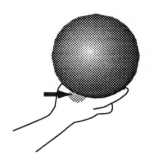

Web of Skin should be neither Taut nor Slack

Figure 9-3

Types of Grips

There are three basic types of grips:

- Conventional Grip;

- Semi Finger-tip Grip

- Finger-tip Grip

With a **conventional grip**, the holes are drilled deeper so that the fingers and thumb enter up to the second knuckle of the hand. With a **semi finger-tip grip**, the holes are drilled so that the fingers fit in up to midway between the second and first knuckles. A **finger-tip grip** is the

Conventional   *Semi Finger-tip*   *Finger-tip*

Figure 9-4

shallowest; the fingers enter only up to the first knuckle.

For new bowlers and those who bowl once a week or less, the conventional grip is the grip of choice.

If you are a frequent bowler and truly want to excel in the sport, adopt a finger-tip grip. This is the grip most of the professionals use. The finger-tip grip will encourage a quicker, smoother thumb and finger release than the conventional release.

We do not recommend the use of the semi finger-tip grip, since it does not allow the hand to contact the bowling ball properly. This is because the finger holes are drilled so the fingers fit in between the knuckles, creating a gap where fingers bend into the holes.

Ball Cover

When we talk about the cover of the ball, we mean the texture or finish. You have probably noticed that some balls have a dull finish while others are shiny. In bowling, this is referred to as **porosity**.

Balls with a high porosity are dull and scratchy, like the surface of an old weather-beaten car. Balls with low porosity are bright and shiny, like the surface of a newly waxed car.

On the lane, balls with different covers will act differently. A dull, high porosity ball will bite-in to the surface of the lane,

provide better traction and hook more. A shiny, low porosity ball will skid more and hook less.

In the last chapter we discussed the different types of lane conditions and how to adjust to them by moving in the stance and using a different type of release. You can also adjust to lane conditions by changing the type of ball you are using.

If the lane conditions are dry, you may be getting more hook than you want. Switching to a shinier, low porosity ball will help reduce this hook.

If the lane conditions are oily, your ball may not be getting enough traction to hook at all. Using a dull, high porosity ball instead will increase traction and your hooking potential.

Remember:

- **Dull, High Porosity Ball**

  ° Better Traction on Lane.

  ° More Hook.

  ° Use on Oily Lanes.

- **Shiny, Low Porosity Ball**

  ° Less Traction on Lane.

  ° More Skidding and Less Hook.

  ° Use on Dry Lanes.

Ball Weight

There are two factors to consider when we talk about ball weight.

The first is the overall weight of the ball. We want you to use a ball that is the proper weight for you.

The second factor is the relationship of the weight block to the thumb and finger holes. Drilling the holes to one side of the weight block instead of centering the holes above the weight block will give the bowling ball more weight on a particular side.

Ball Weight in General

As we mentioned earlier, balls range in weight from six to 16 pounds. Which weight is correct for you?

A general rule of thumb is to **use the heaviest ball you can control without sacrificing accuracy or ball speed.**

When you go to a bowling center or pro shop, try handling balls of different weight. If a ball is too light, you will be able to toss it around easily. If a ball is too heavy, you will feel weighed down and off balance handling it. Once more, comfort is the key.

The Weight Block and Weighting

Many new bowlers hear terms like right side weight, positive weight or finger weight and think that a ball driller adds weight to a bowling ball.

Ball drillers do not add weight to a ball. Instead, they take it out when they drill the holes. From one to three ounces of material are removed when holes are drilled in a ball.

According to ABC/WIBC regulations, the top of a bowling ball can weigh up to three ounces more than the bottom after the holes are drilled. In addition, weight can vary up to one ounce in any direction from center.

Right/Left Side Weight

If the **holes are drilled to the left of the weight block**, there will be more weight on the right hand side. This ball will have **right side weight**.

If the **holes are drilled to the right of the weight block**, there will be more weight on the left hand side. This ball will have **left side weight**.

Balls with right side weight are often referred to as having positive weight. Balls with left side weight are referred to as having negative weight. (This is reversed if you are left-handed.)

If the **holes are drilled directly over top the weight block**, the ball will have **no side weight**. This is the type of ball we recommend for beginners.

Experienced bowlers put right or left side weight on a ball to affect the way it reacts on a lane. This is an advanced bowling technique best used by seasoned bowlers.

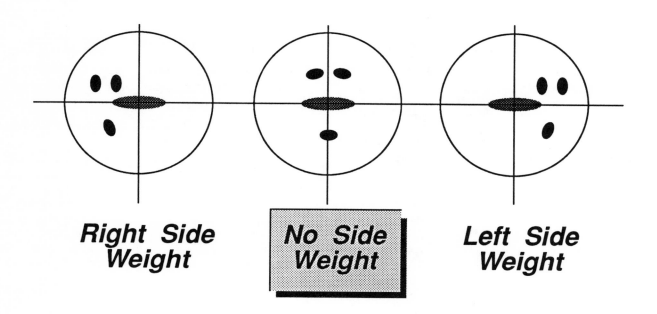

Right Side Weight   *No Side Weight*   *Left Side Weight*

Figure 9-5

Thumb/Finger Weight

If the center of the weight block is closer to the finger holes, a ball has finger weight. If the center of the weight block is closer to the thumb holes, the ball has thumb weight.

Work with a professional ball driller to see which is the best for you.

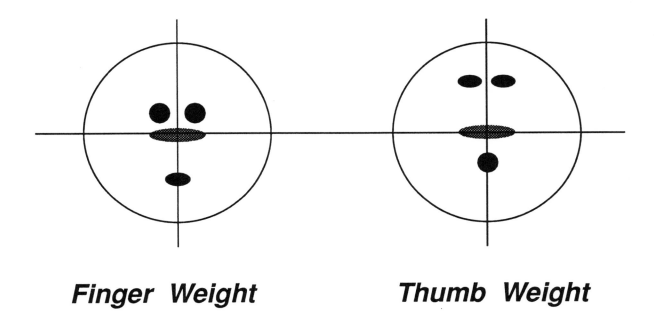

Finger Weight   Thumb Weight

Figure 9-6

Bowling Shoes

There is a difference between the house bowling shoes you rent at the control counter of a bowling center and those you purchase for personal use.

The soles of the shoes you rent are leather on both the right and left feet. Leather soles enable your feet to slide easier when you get to the foul line. The heels are made of white rubber to prevent leaving marks on the approach.

When you get your own personal shoes, only one of the shoes will have a leather sole.

For a **right-handed bowler**, the **sole of the left shoe will be leather**. This is the foot that you plant with during your fourth step as you slide toward the foul line. The other sole will be rubber to give you traction.

(Sometimes the toe of this shoe will have leather on the bottom to help your foot slide sideways in back of the body easier.)

For a **left-handed bowler**, the **sole of the right shoe will be leather**. This is the foot that you plant with during your fourth step as you slide toward to foul line. The other sole will be rubber to give you traction. (Sometimes the toe of this shoe will have leather on the bottom to help your foot slide sideways in back of the body easier.)

Note: In this chapter we have covered the basics of bowling balls and shoes. For those who want to learn more about how using different balls can improve your game, we recommend reading **Bowling: Knowledge is the Key**.

Chapter Ten

Mastering the Mental Game

Overview

Bowling is a singular sport. Even in league competition, when a person gets up to bowl it's only the bowler versus the pins. Perhaps this is why the mental elements of sports and competition play such an important role in bowling.

When we talk about the mental game of bowling, we are covering many different aspects.

For example, some people become depressed if they don't see dramatic improvement all at once. As with many other areas in life, progress in bowling happens in stages, with long plateaus in between.

Other people try so hard to remember everything they need to do that they "over-think" the game. Often, bowlers become too excited or "psyched-out" before a big game. Conversely, others lack motivation, enthusiasm and energy for a variety of reasons.

After the physical skills of bowling have been acquired, mastering the mind and the mental game is the next step. In this chapter we will discuss methods to help boost your confidence, avoid over-thinking, develop positive mental images, and become psyched-up instead of psyched-out.

These techniques are useful for more than bowling or even sports in general. They can help you lead a happier life, reduce stress and anxiety, and succeed in any endeavor of your life.

Note: The majority of this material has been provided by the United States Olympic Committee Elite Coaches Workshop in Sports Psychology. We thank the US Olympic Committee for their permission to use this information and the opportunity to attend these workshops. They were very helpful to our sport.

Competence = Confidence

People feel good about doing the things they do well. As your skill increases, your mental attitude toward the game will improve as well.

Confidence comes when you know you have what it takes to get the job done. When you have mastered the basics of bowling. When you know how to adjust to lane conditions and dial into the strike pocket. When adjusting for a difficult spare conversion is a reflex action.

And mastering these techniques can only come through practice.

Make Bowling Fun!

The term "practice" conjures up images of an individual performing the same boring task over and over again. This is not the case in bowling. Every time you get up to bowl you are faced with a different set of challenges. The lane conditions will be different than the last time. You will be different. That's the challenge of bowling. And part of the fun!

Don't get so wrapped up in improving your game that you forget to enjoy the sport. We strongly recommend that new bowlers join a league where they can make new friends, improve their game, and have a lot of fun at the same time.

Positive Self Talk

Each of us has a little voice inside that talks to us. What is that voice saying to you? Are you receiving positive or negative reinforcement?

What your inner voice says to you has a great effect on your mental attitude. While it is true that you can be your own worst critic, make sure that you are giving yourself positive suggestions and not negative criticism.

We recommend that you make a tape for yourself. Record some music on it that makes you feel good. And actually talk to yourself on this tape. Remind yourself that you are improving. Review past achievements that made you feel proud. Fantasize about future improvements and achievements.

Remember: You are what you think.

Positive Mental Imagery

Mental Imagery is a more intense form of internal communication than self talk. Think of mental imagery as a vivid daydream.

Most forms of mental imagery are playbacks from our memory. Mental images can seem so real that all the senses are engaged. In very vivid images, the visual, auditory, tactile (touch), olfactory (smells and taste), and kinesthetic (body movement and motion) senses all become involved.

Mental imagery can be so vivid that thousands of minute details are visualized at once. Think about lining up in the stance and making a shot. This can be visualized in one vivid mental image, although it takes thousands of words to describe it in a book.

Everyone experiences mental imagery in some form. Recently, however, researchers have learned to develop mental imagery into a powerful tool for improving skill, generating positive mental attitudes, and increasing one's drive and energy.

There are two types of mental imagery.

- **Goal-oriented imagery** involves developing mental images of success. It can be an image as complex as bowling strike after strike, finally making that 300 game and hearing the roar of the crowd in the background. Or it can be a simple image, such as converting a difficult spare.

- **Process imagery** involves imagining the physical process itself. This is a great way to supplement your actual practice sessions and improve.

Why Imagery Works

There are four basic reasons why practicing imagery helps athletes perform better.

- When you relive a moment or daydream, the brain actually sends signals to the appropriate muscles. These signals are called neuromuscular impulses. They are weaker versions of the same neuromuscular impulses that make your muscles work. When you imagine yourself bowling, you are actually strengthening the neural pathways!

- Practicing imagery "programs" your mind with a set of instructions so that during an actual game the movements are more familiar and therefore more natural.

- Imagery helps you maintain your emotional peak. When practicing imagery, you imagine yourself being successful and doing everything perfectly. This helps you achieve a positive mental attitude geared toward success while alleviating feelings of stress and depression.

- When used just before competition, imagery prepares the mind and body to work while clearing away negative thoughts and distractions. **In effect, it replaces worrying with positive mental images, boosting your confidence.**

Practicing Imagery

Imagery is a skill that takes practice to develop. The more you practice mental imagery, the easier it becomes. The mental images will also become more vivid.

Here are a few hints to help you practice mental imagery.

- Combine imagery practice with actual practice. They will reinforce each other.

- Practice imagery when you are alone in a quiet place. Outside influences will interfere with your "daydreaming" and weaken the effect. With practice, however, you will find that you can practice imagery even in a crowd. This should be your goal.

- Practice imagery in conjunction with self-hypnosis, relaxation or meditation. This will help focus your attention, as well as making the mental images more vivid.

Relaxation and Breathing

The techniques we just described are more effective when combined with various relaxation and breathing techniques. Relaxation techniques help focus your mind on what you are doing.

In addition, relaxation — when practiced just before an actual game — will relieve stress and anxiety, allowing you to bowl your best.

There are many different relaxation techniques. Any of these techniques may be used to put your mind and body in a deep relaxation state. The following method is similar to one that has been successfully used by Team USA bowlers and other athletes at the United States Olympic Training Center.

1. Find a quiet place where you can be alone and relaxed for 10 or 15 minutes.

2. Lie on your back. Place you hands by your side. Keep your legs straight, not crossed. As soon as you are comfortable, close your eyes.

3. Begin breathing deeply and slowly. Make sure to use your diaphragm when you breath. You'll know that you are breathing deeply with your diaphragm when your stomach — not your chest — begins to rise and fall slowly.

    Take a deep breath, hold it in for a few seconds, then slowly let it out. It may be helpful to breath in with your nose and out with your mouth.

    After a minute or two, you will notice that both mind and body are moving toward a more relaxed state.

4. Try to visualize with your mind one of your feet. When you can "see with your mind," concentrate on relaxing all of the muscles in the foot.

    For example, you may say to yourself, "My foot is becoming heavy, heavy with relaxation. I can feel all the muscles loosening and relaxing."

    Don't try to concentrate too hard, or you will "over-think" and actually generate the anxiety you are trying to relieve. Let it happen naturally. Remember that these techniques take practice in order to fully master them.

    If you feel any anxiety, stop, concentrate on your breathing and let your mind naturally drop back into a relaxed state.

5. Relax the muscles the other foot in the same way, then one leg, then the other leg. Continue slowly up the body until you are totally relaxed and in an even deeper mental state.

6. In this deeply relaxed state, your mind will be much more receptive to suggestion than during normal consciousness. This is the best time to practice Self Talk and Mental Imagery. Remember, you don't have to do it for long. A few minutes a day is sufficient.

7. When finished, concentrate once more on your breathing. Stretch your arms and legs slowly. Then open your eyes.

The use of breathing as a relaxation technique can also be used during a game. The next time you feel stress or anxiety, stop, take a few deep breaths and let your mind clear. You will automatically feel more relaxed.

Mentally Preparing for a Game

Preparing for a game starts before you even get to the bowling center. Obviously proper sleep the night before is one of the best ways to prepare your mind and body to perform at top proficiency. As far as eating, don't be hungry or full, but somewhere in between.

Listen to your self-talk tape on the way to the bowling center, and visualize yourself going out there and playing your best.

When you get to the bowling center, get a feel for the condition of the lane. Start planning how you will adjust to the lane if your first impressions are confirmed.

Before you get up to bowl, imagine a circular area somewhere between the ball return and the scoring table. This will be your **think circle** where you will wait when you are the next person up to bowl.

When in the think circle, visualize what you will do, from lining up into the stance to ending up in the finish position. Imagine the ball following that "Line in Your Mind."

Then, when it's your turn, align yourself in the stance and **do it without hesitation**. Once you line up in the stance, the time for thinking is over. Your decisions have already been made in the think circle. If you think in the stance, you may "over-think" and end up psyching yourself out.

Practice the techniques in this chapter and you will soon realize improvement in not only your bowling score but your overall mental attitude as well.

Afterword

Where to Go from Here

Perhaps the biggest reason for bowling's popularity is that it can be enjoyed on many different levels. Bowling is an excellent form of family recreation. All members of the family, from grandparents to toddlers and everyone in between, can have fun in a wholesome, family-oriented environment. For weekly enthusiasts, leagues provide opportunities for adults and adolescents to relax and socialize while enjoying the excitement and challenge of competition. For those who want to progress further, there is no limit. Top professional bowlers earn over $200,000 a year in prize winnings, not counting revenues from product endorsements and guest appearances. And at the amateur level, Team USA represents this country in international competition with over 80 different countries.

Perhaps the first step for a new bowler is to join a league. There are three national bowling organizations who coordinate bowling leagues on a nationwide basis.

National Bowling Organizations

There are two national bowling associations for adult league bowlers. The **American Bowling Congress (ABC)** is the official governing body for men's league bowling. The **Women's International Bowling Congress (WIBC)** is the national governing body for women's league bowling.

In addition to overseeing league functions, these organizations monitor other aspects of the sport. ABC and WIBC are responsible for developing and enforcing regulations concerning lanes, bowling balls, record-keeping, and league and tournament conduct. A variety of research projects are carried out by ABC/WIBC at the test facilities of the World Bowling Headquarters. In addition, these organizations bond leagues to protect league funds from misuse or theft, and provide leagues with all necessary operating supplies. ABC/WIBC also coordinates numerous public relations, promotional and educational programs.

For youths and teenagers, the **Young American Bowling Alliance (YABA)** coordinates league competition. YABA also trains coaches and develops educational programs for public schools, colleges and countless other projects.

The organization for professional male bowlers is the **Professional Bowlers Association (PBA)**. The PBA is the governing body for the national bowling tour. You have no doubt seen televised PBA tournaments on major networks.

The organization for professional female bowlers is the **Ladies Pro Bowlers Tour (LPBT)**. LPBT tournaments are also televised nationally.

The **United States Tenpin Bowling Federation (USTBF)** is the official national governing body of amateur bowling. USTBF funds and oversees **Team USA**, the official bowling team representing the United States. This organization also develops and conducts coaching certification programs as well as bowling clinics for beginning, intermediate and advanced bowlers.

United States Tenpin Bowling Federation

The United States
National Amateur
Bowling Tournament

Federation Internationale des Quilleurs (FIQ) is the international governing body of bowling. Over 100 million people bowl in the 70+ countries comprising FIQ! Member countries of FIQ compete against each other in global competition during such events as the FIQ World Tournament, Pan American Games, the Goodwill Games and the 1988 Olympics in Seoul, Korea.

Most bowling centers in the country belong to the **Bowling Proprietors Association of America (BPAA)**. The BPAA sponsors national advertising and public relation campaigns, conducts training programs for employees of bowling centers, functions as a lobbying arm to promote the interests of the sport, and sponsors a variety of national youth, adult and professional tournaments.

Selected representatives of all the national organizations we just mentioned — as well as representatives from all major bowling manufacturers — belong to the **National Bowling Council (NBC)**. Headquartered in Washington, D.C., the NBC funds and coordinates a broad range of marketing, market research, public relations, advertising and educational programs.

National Bowling Council

Further Development

This book has provided you with the all of the information you need to improve your game and master the basic skills of bowling.

For those who wish to progress further, we recommend reading **Bowling: Knowledge is the Key**. This book covers such information as reading lanes, advanced physical adjustments, three additional releases and advanced lane adjustments. Hundreds of professional bowlers, including national titleholders, have benefited from the information in this book.

Many bowling centers also offer bowling clinics. In these clinics, seasoned bowling coaches can help you trouble-shoot and correct your game.

Bowling Concepts also provides a video analysis service called **The Coach's Eye**.

We can evaluate your game utilizing a video tape of you bowling. If you are interested in this individualized program, contact Bowling Concepts at (216) 762- 8683 for more information.

We wish you all the best of luck in your bowling career, whether it becomes a once-a-week diversion or your full-time profession. Remember: once you know what to do, all that remains is to practice until the techniques are yours. And **you will improve**. Bowling has always attracted positive people, who have what it takes to succeed.

Appendix A

Keeping Score

Many first-time bowlers are confused about keeping score. While scoring in bowling may appear difficult, once a few basic points are understood, it's as easy as keeping score in any other sport.

Automatic scorekeepers, now common in many bowling centers, have taken a lot of the work out of keeping score. But it's still important to know a few basic points.

Basics of Scoring

In bowling, a **game** consists of **ten frames**. During a **frame**, you get **two chances to knock down all the pins**. If you **knock down all the pins the first time, you don't take your second shot**, but instead go on to the next frame.

When you bowl a frame, three things can happen.

- **Strike:** A strike is when you **knock down all the pins on your first shot of** a frame.

- **Spare:** A spare is when you **knock down all the pins in two shots.**

- **Open:** An **open frame** means that **there are still pins standing** after you take your two shots.

Note: You may have heard the term "split." With a split, after the first shot, there are pins standing in such a way that it is difficult for you to knock the remainder down in the next shot. In other words, you will have to either aim between the remaining pins or skid one pin into the other(s) in order to knock them down.

Whether a shot is a split or not has nothing to do with the score. If you knock down the remaining pins, you'll have a spare; if you don't, you'll have an open frame.

Scoring in bowling gives you extra "rewards" or bonuses if you knock down all the pins in a frame. If you knock them all down on the first shot of a frame (a strike) you get an opportunity to make more "bonus" points than if it takes two shots (a spare).

Here's how it works:

- An open frame is worth the **number of pins you knocked down** in the frame.

- A **spare** is worth **ten points plus your next shot.**

- A **strike** is worth **ten points plus your next two shots.**

The Scorecard

Figure A-1 shows a sample scorecard.

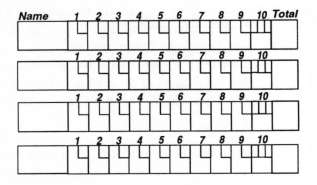

Figure A-1

On each line of the scorecard, one bowler can keep score of a game.

Notice that there are ten large squares on every line. These squares represent the ten frames you bowl in a game.

In the right hand corner of each of the first nine frames, there is a smaller square. In the tenth frame, though, notice that there are three squares running along the top. This is because the tenth or last frame of a game differs somewhat from the first nine.

For now, let's concentrate on the first nine frames. Figure A-2 shows a sample frame on a score card.

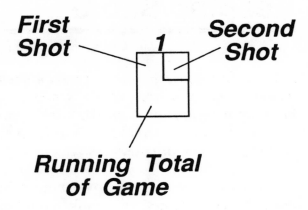

Figure A-2

Briefly, here's how to score a frame:

- Record the pins you knock down on your first shot to the left of the little square.

- If you bowl an open frame, record the pins you knock down on your second shot in the little square to the right. This is also where you write the strike (X) and spare (/) symbols.

- Keep a running total of the game in the bottom portion of the frame.

For example, suppose on the first shot of the first frame you knock down six pins. On the next shot, you knock down two pins. The first frame would be scored as in Figure A-3.

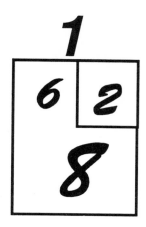

Figure A-3

Symbols Used on the Scorecard

There are four basic symbols that are used on the scorecard:

- If you make a **strike**, put a large "**X**" in the little square. (There's no need to write "10" to the left of the square, because the "X" means that you knocked down all ten pins on your first try.)

Figure A-4

Notice that we didn't put any score in the "running total" area in the bottom of the frame. This is because a strike is worth ten pins plus the next two shots. You can't record the running total for this frame until you have made two more shots.

- If you make a **spare**, put a slash "/" in the little square. Also, record the pins you knocked down on the first shot to the left of the little square. (There's no need to record your score of the second shot, since the slash mark indicates that you knocked down the remaining pins.)

Figure A-5

As with the example of a strike, we have not filled-in the "running total" in Figure A-5. This is because a spare is worth ten points plus the next shot. You can't fill-in the running total until you have made one more shot.

- If you **miss all the pins during a shot**, record a dash "—". If you miss all the pins during your first shot, put the dash to the left of the little square; if you miss all the pins during the second shot, put the dash inside the little square.

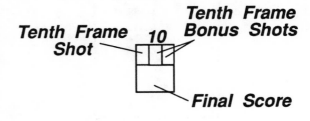

Figure A-7

The tenth frame is a little different than the other frames. In the tenth frame, you can get up to three shots. That's why there are three little squares in this frame.

Figure A-6

Note: You may have noticed that sometimes a bowler will circle the number to the right of the little square. This indicates that the bowler was left with a split for the second shot. Use of the circle has nothing to do with actual scoring. It just signifies a difficult spare shot.

The reason that the tenth frame is different is because you have to be able to finish out the game. Let's suppose you make a strike in the tenth frame. According to the scoring rules of bowling, a strike is worth ten points plus the next two shots. But there are no more frames to be played; the tenth frame is the last. That's why you have the opportunity to make up to two extra shots during the tenth frame.

The Tenth Frame

Here are the general rules:

Figure A-7 shows the tenth frame of a scorecard.

- If you make a **strike during the tenth frame,** you get **two extra shots.**

- If you make a **spare during the tenth frame,** you get **one extra shot.**

- If you **open** or leave pins standing **during the tenth frame**, you get **no extra shots**.

A few examples should help clarify this.

Example One

Suppose that you begin the tenth frame with a score of 150. On your first shot, you get a strike. This means you get two more chances. On your next shot, you get a nine, and you miss the remaining pin on your final shot. The final two frames would look like this.

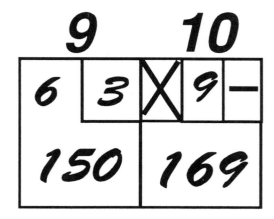

Figure A-8

Notice that adding up your shots on the final **tenth frame** is simple. You just **add them all up!**

Example Two

In this example, your score in the ninth frame is 160. On your first shot in the tenth frame, you get nine. On your next shot you get the remaining pin, earning a spare. In a normal frame, that would be it, but in the tenth frame, you get another shot. On this shot, you get nine. Your total in the tenth frame is 19, which added to 160 gives you a final score of 179.

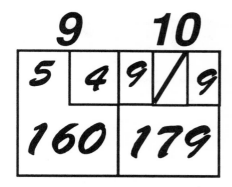

Figure A-9

Note: Notice that in this example there is still a pin left standing at the end of the game. In this case, before another person can bowl you will have to use the reset button on the return to set up the pins for the next player.

Example Three

This time you enter the tenth frame with a score of 165. On your first shot you get eight. On your next shot, you get one, leaving a pin. This means you have an open frame in the tenth. There is no extra shot. Your score for the tenth frame is nine, giving you a final score of 174.

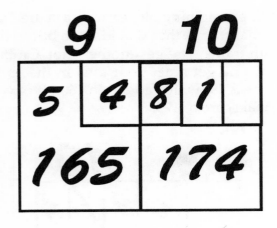

Figure A-10

Scoring a Sample Game

This sample game will demonstrate everything we have discussed previously. If you can follow the steps frame-by-frame, you will have no difficulty scoring your own game.

In the **First Frame**, you bowl a spare. Notice we have not filled in a score for the frame, because you have to bowl another shot first.

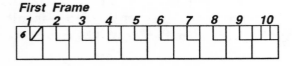

Figure A-11

In the **Second Frame**, you bowl a strike. The ten from this shot is added to the ten from the first frame to give you a score of twenty in the First Frame. We have not filled in a score for the Second Frame, because you have to bowl the next two shots first.

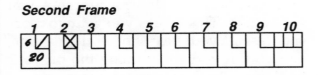

Figure A-12

In the **Third Frame**, you make eight on your first shot, then miss the remaining pins on your second shot. We can now fill in the Second Frame (20+10+8=38) and the Third Frame (38+8=46).

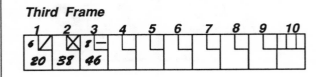

Figure A-13

Since you're beginning to warm up, you bowl strikes in the **Fourth** and **Fifth Frames**. Figure A-14 shows how we have indicated strikes for these frames, but have not filled-in the scores yet since a strike is worth ten points plus the next two shots.

Fourth and Fifth Frames

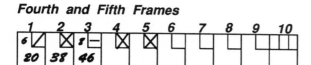

Figure A-14

In the **Sixth Frame**, you bowl a nine in the first shot, then pick up the remaining pin for a spare. Now we can fill in the running totals for Frame Four (46+10+10+9=75) and Frame Five (75+10+9+1=95)

Sixth Frame

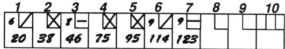

Figure A-15

In the **Seventh Frame**, you knock down nine pins on your first shot, then miss the last pin on the second shot. We can now fill in the running totals for Frame Six (95+10+9=114) and Frame Seven (114+9=123)

Seventh Frame

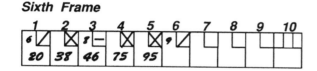

Figure A-16

In the **Eighth** and **Ninth Frames**, you bowl strikes. Notice in Figure A-17 we have indicated these strikes but have not filled in any running totals, since we can't yet.

Eighth and Ninth Frames

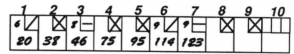

Tenth Frame

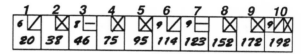

Figure A-17

In the first shot of the **Tenth Frame**, you knock down nine pins. Now we can fill in running total for the Eighth Frame (123+10+10+9=152). On your next shot, you knock down the remaining pin and make the spare. Now we can fill in the running total for the Ninth Frame (152+10+9+1=172).

Since it is the Tenth Frame and you have made a spare, you take your extra shot and make a strike. Now you can add up the three shots of the Tenth Frame and get your final game score (172+9+1+10=192).

300: The Perfect Game

The highest score you can get in bowling is 300. To attain a 300 game, you must bowl

12 consecutive strikes. Figure A-18 shows a scorecard for a perfect 300 game. As we just did in the sample, track this game frame by frame to see how we arrived at a 300 score.

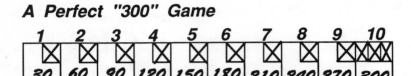

Figure A-18

Appendix B

Leagues and Tournaments

As we have said before, perhaps the most exciting part of bowling is competing in leagues and tournaments. The ABC, WIBC and YABA coordinate league activities at thousands of bowling centers in the United States. Leagues organized by these national associations are called "sanctioned leagues."

In addition to sanctioned league competition, there is sanctioned tournament competition. These tournaments are organized at the local, state and national level. There are different tournaments for different classes of bowlers, so even beginning bowlers can enjoy the thrill of one-on-one competition in a tournament.

Because of the handicap system used by leagues, new bowlers can compete successfully in any sanctioned league. The handicap system provides newer bowlers with lower averages a "head start" by giving them handicap points before the game even starts.

There are also tournaments that give newer bowlers handicap points so they can compete one-on-one with bowlers whose averages are far higher.

Joining a League

To join a league all you have to do is call your local bowling center. Someone at the control counter will be happy to assist you. Fall/Winter leagues usually start around Labor Day and last 12-36 weeks. Summer leagues run from May to August.

Almost all the tedious work is handled by the league secretary. The league secretary keeps all of your personal and team records, figures out your averages and handicaps each week, schedules the teams you will play and what lane you will use, and posts team and individual standings. All of this information will be posted on the bulletin board at the bowling center.

All you have to do is show up each week, check the bulletin board, bowl the best you can and pay your dues.

Make sure you are matched with people whose company you enjoy. Ask someone at the control desk or even the bowling proprietor personally what league would be the best for you. After all, the bowling proprietor really has one goal: to make sure you enjoy yourself and keep coming back.

For single people there are mixed leagues; for couples there are couples leagues; and, there are numerous men's and women's leagues. There are also many special interest leagues. These include senior citizens, career/vocational, PTA and local school leagues. The nice part about special interest leagues is that you know you will be in the company of those who share common interests with you.

Also make sure you are matched with bowlers who are close in ability to you. Most bowling centers have one or more league(s) comprised of top notch bowlers. Even though the extra handicap points will help you out, you probably won't enjoy bowling a 120 game when all around you are bowling 180 or better. Ask around the bowling center and find out which leagues are for newer players.

Also, make sure you get along well with your team members. Nothing can ruin the fun of bowling more than conflict between teammates. The safest bet is to talk some of your friends into joining with you, then start your own team.

Above all, don't feel self-conscious about having a low average at first. The lower your average, the more handicap points you will get as a head start. Also, as a new

player you will improve much faster than seasoned teammates. These two factors will make you a real asset to your team.

The Handicap System

As we mentioned, league competition is based upon a handicap system. The handicap system spots bowlers with lower averages extra points. It's like getting a head start before the game even begins.

You really don't need to understand that much about handicaps because your league secretary will calculate your new average and handicap every week you bowl. It is helpful, though, to understand what is going on behind the scenes.

When you bowl on a league your average is calculated by the league secretary each week. Your average is a running total of all your scores divided by the number of games you have bowled that season. This means that if you start bowling better each week, your average will go up. When you start a new season, your beginning average is the average you had the previous year.

Example

	Game 1	Game 2	Game 3	Weekly Total	Grand Total	
WEEK I	112	107	122	341	341	113.8
WEEK II	123	109	133	365	706	117.4

Example of Calculating Averages

A handicap is based on a percentage of the difference between your team average and the average of the other team. This percentage is usually between 70% and 90%. (In the following example, we will use the 90% handicap system.)

A team can have anywhere from 2-5 players on it. In this example, let's assume that you have five players on your team.

Your Team

Player 1 Average = 140

Player 2 Average = 135

Player 3 Average = 120

Player 4 Average = 115

Player 5 Average = 130

Total Team Average = 640

Team USA, the official bowling team representing the United States, happens to be in town and wants to play your team in their first exhibition game! This is their current team average:

Team USA

Player 1 Average = 225

Player 2 Average = 210

Player 3 Average = 215

Player 4 Average = 220

Player 5 Average = 210

Total Team Average = 1080

The **difference between the two team averages is 440 points** (1080-640=440).

Assuming that you are playing with the 90% handicap system, you would multiply the difference by 90% to determine your handicap:

(440X90%=**396**).

This means that before you even begin the game you will start out with a head start of 396 points. The starting score will be Your Team: 396 points; Team USA: 0.

Handicap, Scratch and Bracket Tournaments

Sanctioned ABC/WIBC tournaments are a great way to enjoy the thrill of one-on-one competition.

There are three basic types of tournaments:

- **Handicap Tournaments**: In a handicap tournament, you will receive a handicap based upon the difference between your bowling average and your opponent's.

  Suppose you have an average of 150 and the person you are bowling against has an average of 190. The difference is 40 pins. If this is a 90% handicap tournament, you will be spotted 36 points before the match even begins!

  A handicap tournament is a great opportunity for a new bowler to win. As a new bowler, it's much easier for you to throw a couple extra strikes and bowl 100 pins over your average than it is for a 200 bowler to bowl 100 pins over his or her average!

- **Scratch Tournaments**: In scratch tournaments, there are no handicaps. The final points at the end of the match are all that count.

- **Bracket Tournaments**: In bracket tournaments, you only compete against those whose averages are close to yours. In others words, there will be divisions, such as a 100-115 division, a 115-130 division, and so on.

Some bracket tournaments are closed to only those individuals who have a certain average. For example, there are tournaments only for players whose averages are over 180; conversely, there are tournaments only for players whose averages are under 180.

Remember: There's prize money to be won at a tournament, and you could be the winner! Sometimes even local tournaments offer top prizes in the thousands of dollars. If you compete in state or national tournaments, you also get the opportunity to travel and see new places.